SARAH BERNHARDT

SARAH BERNHARDT

WILLIAM EMBODEN
Introduction by Sir John Gielgud

Macmillan Publishing Co., Inc.
New York

For my mother
'La Grande . . .'

Acknowledgements

I especially wish to thank Miss Elizabeth Coates and Miss Josephine Hickey who worked so tirelessly on this manuscript. Institutions cooperating with this research are:

    La Cinémathèque Française, Paris
    The Academy of Motion Picture Arts and Sciences (Los Angeles)
    The Museum of Modern Art (Film Archives), New York
    La Phonothèque Nationale, Paris
    The University of California, Los Angeles (Special Collections Library).

The author wishes to thank the following for permission to reproduce photographs in the text. Unacknowledged photographs and objects are in the author's collection and while every effort has been made to trace their original ownership, no source has been found.
Acknowledgements for illustrations pages 82, 87, 149, 154, 162, 163 H. Roger-Viollet, Paris; pages 15, 39 bottom, 52, 71 top, 73, 80, 81 left Nadar Collection, Archives Photographiques, Paris; page 83 SPADEM, Paris; pages 31, 42 Ferrers Gallery, London; front of jacket Duane Wakeham, California; pages 59, 60, 109, 147 The Museum of Modern Art, Film Stills Archive, New York.

Macmillan Publishing Co. Inc.,
866 Third Avenue, New York, N.Y. 10022

Library of Congress Catalog Card Number: 75-685

First published in Great Britain in 1974 by Studio Vista
First American edition 1975

Printed in Great Britain

Contents

'You ask me my theory of life. It is represented by the word *will* . . . Life is short, even for those of us who live a long time, and we must live for the few who know and appreciate us, who judge and absolve us, and for whom we have the same affection and indulgence. We ought to hate very rarely, as it is too fatiguing, remain indifferent a great deal, forgive often, and never forget.'

Sarah Bernhardt
The Daily Telegraph
London 28 March 1923

Introduction

Can we, in this generation, have any idea what she was really like, this Rosine Bernard, the little girl who was to become the great actress Sarah Bernhardt – Sarah Barnum (as someone unkindly called her), Queen of Sardoodledom, destined to sway the audiences of two continents for nearly fifty years, the Sacred Monster whose name – with those of her great contemporary rivals, Ellen Terry and Eleanora Duse – was to ring triumphantly through half the nineteenth century and was still a household word in the first twenty years of this one?

The photographs in this book give us a remarkable opportunity to see her in many moods and impersonations, as she gradually develops from a romantic, neurotic, young actress into the statuesque, imposing, matron of middle age. Only at the very end does she appear to submit to the ravages of time, more tragically crippled than the tragic heroines she had played so long.

We follow her through these pictures in her great procession of Queens, Princesses, adventuresses and courtesans as well as some of her strange transvestite excursions. As Hamlet, ('très grande dame' was Max Beerbohm's comment) Lorenzáccio, Pelleas, and the boy L'Aiglon, Napoleon's son, a rôle she created when she was already fifty-six years old.

She glowers at us as Théodora, writhes as Cleopatra, coquettes as Tosca, scowls above her highnecked collar as a silent-film Queen Elizabeth, yearns and swoons as Marguerite Gauthier in 'La Dame aux Camélias', the old melodrama which our parents and grandparents

7

thought so shockingly improper that they would only go to see it when it was played in French. The part was probably Sarah's own favourite. It was certainly the most popular in her repertoire, whenever she appeared in it all over the world.

Fantastic, formidable creature, quite as spectacular in her private (or should one say public) life as in the theatre!

Sleeping in her coffin, nursing the wounded during the siege of Paris, flying over the city in a balloon, fencing, sculpting, painting, driving her lovers to fight duels for her favours, and her managers to bring lawsuits against her.

Later on, when she goes into management, she directs her own plays, selects her companies and authors, takes pupils (giving them lessons and small parts in her plays to gain experience), and, whenever she is not appearing in Paris, tours untiringly all over Europe and America. In the States she travels across to the West Coast in her own special train, and when she quarrels with the management of a theatre she has booked, acts in a tent, a tabernacle or a skating rink where audiences flock to see her. She takes an occasional holiday at her house in Belle-Isle, where she tries to play tennis and live as a country chatelaine while entertaining a house-party and planning her next production. She makes huge sums of money and squanders it with spectacular generosity.

At last, when she is getting old, Fate turns against her, and she has to have one of her legs amputated above the knee. To everyone's amazement she insists on going back to work, is carried by car and chair to the Front where she recites to the troops, and continues to act during the last five years remaining to her, giving, both in America and in London, short scenes from her repertoire and half-hour playlets in which she does not need to move.

It was in one of these that I was lucky enough to see her, when I was thirteen years old, at the London Coliseum. She played the part of a young French poilu, lying mortally wounded on a bank in a wood near the battle-field. I remember so well how she looked in her short brown wig, her horizon-blue tunic open at the neck, and the lower half of her body covered with a rug. In her right hand she grasped a tattered flag, and during the course of the action she recited some patriotic verses, after which she fell back dead. I understood very few of the words she spoke, but there was a magical stillness in the big auditorium, and her voice rang out, throbbing with energy and varying modulations of rhythm and colour. The curtain fell, but rose again almost immediately to reveal her standing proudly upright on her one leg, leaning her hand on the shoulder of one of her fellow actors for support. I was spellbound.

Esmé Percy, who had been a member of her company when he was a young man, used to tell me fascinating tales about her – how he would find her sitting before her mirror beginning to make-up, muttering gracious asides to herself as if she was acknowledging the homage of an invisible group of attendant courtiers ranged around her. And how, if the audience was arriving late, chattering and inattentive, she was immediately aware of it, and would deliberately delay her entrance (already carefully worked-up) and remain behind the scenes, while the unfortunate actors who opened the play were obliged to maintain the necessary suspense by somewhat inept improvisations of dialogue. 'Ah, écoute, elle arrive, la princesse!' 'Non, non, elle n'arrive pas encore.'

Was she really a great actress, or merely a great star personality with a genius for publicity and showmanship? She seems like Henry Irving – whom she admired more as an artist than as an actor (and perhaps one might say the opposite of Sarah herself) – to have adored claptrap and believed in it utterly, knowing of course that her most obviously melodramatic performances would appeal most strongly to audiences who did not speak her language. Lady Macbeth and Cleopatra were not among her successes, though she essayed both parts. Phèdre, on the other hand, was admitted by nearly all her critics to be a superb classical performance and the high spot of her career, but she chose to play it very seldom in her later years.

. She must have had an inspired sense of occasion, a flair for presentation, an iron constitution (though in her youth she was considered extremely delicate) and a consummate technique which served her well when she was tired or bored or at odds with her public – which seems to have been a very rare occurrence. Sometimes she lacked taste, thirsted for publicity, thrived on sensational exhibitionism, and she was evidently shrewd, apt to be jealous, vain and even childish, particularly in her sense of humour. One cannot fail to be shocked, even while one is amused, at her successful efforts to outdo the redoubtable Mrs Patrick Campbell in fooling on the stage, squashing a raw egg into the palm of her hand during a tender love-scene and tying a property goldfish to the bottom of Melisande's well. But Mrs Campbell herself paid tribute to her after her death in an article she wrote in New York in 1937.

> 'The more classic the rôle, the more wonderful was her timing, the more marvellous the management of her voice, as though some deep courtesy within herself towards her audience insisted that the beauty and sense of every word she spoke must be understood and felt.'

9

Ruthlessly ambitious, sometimes ridiculous, holding court among her friends, colleagues, lovers, and menagerie of animals, she seems to us now impossible, outrageous and somewhat terrifying. Devoted to Irving and Ellen Terry, jealously tolerant of Duse, she worshipped a scapegrace son, married a dope-fiend who deserted her, and indulged in a series of notorious love affairs at different times in her long career.

But surely it was her work that always came before everything else. She was an out-and-out professional to the very end. In the week before she died she tried to finish a film in which she had promised to take the part of an old fortune-teller. She was already so ill that one of the rooms in her house had to be adapted as a studio, and there she faced the cameras for the last time. Many years before she had played in England (Sir George Arthur tells the story), before the Duchess of Teck, the mother of the late Queen Mary. After the performance she was presented, and the Duchess asked if she were not tired out.

'Altesse Royale', said Madame Bernhardt, throwing back her head, 'Je mourrai en scène; c'est mon champ de bataille.'

Sir John Gielgud, March 1974

Author's Preface

'The secret of that astounding utterance baffles the imagination.
The words boomed and crashed with a superhuman resonance which
shook the hearer like a leaf in the wind . . . there was more than gold,
there was thunder and lightning, there was heaven and hell.'
                              Lytton Strachey, Century Magazine, 1923.
                              Commenting on Sarah Bernhardt.

Who was Sarah Bernhardt? It would be far too simple to say that she
was the greatest actress of the last century, for she was more than an
actress, and belongs to more than one century. She was born in 1844,
and as a child her ambition was to spend her life in a convent, for
although her mother was Jewish, Sarah was converted to Catholicism
at an early age. Had it not been for her mother's insistence, the young
Sarah would never have seen the inside of a theatre. Her tears of
protest at being forced into the sinful atmosphere of the Odéon in
Paris instead of the romantic Saint Sulpice, were soon dried by a
succession of performances that were to lead to her début in the
Comédie Française while she was still in her teens. As the actress
matured to fit her rôles, the voice grew in volume, colour and tone.
Every major playwright welcomed a chance to write for her. Among
them, Oscar Wilde wrote his *Salomé* in French purely as a vehicle for
her talent. At the age of thirty-six, she launched a world tour, during
which she achieved the daunting task of conquering English-speaking
peoples everywhere with performances presented in French. Her
memoirs in two volumes enthralled French, English and Americans

11

alike. They present a portrait of this great woman at the height of her success not only as an actress, but also as a writer, a sculptor, a painter, and a great humanitarian. A woman who was born an illegitimate Jewess in a Paris fraught with antisemitism, who was abandoned by her mother as a child, who was told when she was young that she was ugly, in spite of it all became the great figure that was to dominate the stage world for decades. La Grande Sarah was slight in stature, barely over five feet in height, but she was commanding in any gathering. Never short on courage, she took a wild balloon trip over Paris, flew in one of the first vestiges of an aeroplane, kept wild animals, and went to San Quentin Prison in 1913, performing for the prisoners, and mingling fearlessly among them.

Little has been said about her career as a writer: apart from the famous memoirs she wrote several plays, a novel, and a children's book (which was based upon her own balloon trip and illustrated by the artist Clairin) and rewrote the plays of others. She contributed columns to newspapers on women's clothing, manners and morals, and *Le Globe* printed her theatrical reviews.

The few reproductions that remain of her one-woman shows of sculpture in Paris and London indicate some talent for Art Nouveau figures. These works rarely come on to the art market now and when they do they fetch thousands of dollars. Many of her pieces were monumental in size and concept, and she immortalized in clay her favourite playwrights, including Sardou, Hugo and Rostand.

When necessary, she could turn her hand to almost anything, sing, dance, play the piano and guitar, she even played tennis. When Le Fèbre needed a frontispiece for his book on the Comédie Française Madame Bernhardt launched into etching and produced a handsome illustration. When war broke out she became a nurse and almost died of starvation because she gave her food to the soldiers.

In 1915 after a series of accidents to her right knee which eventually became gangrenous, she had her leg amputated, and yet within months she was at the front lines performing for the French troops. In order to pay her way and to keep up an extravagant style of life she worked to the very end, when well into her seventies she was sadly misused by American vaudville theatres. She was even filmed on her deathbed in March 1923.

Cylinders and discs of her golden voice have become rare, and films are to be found in only a few archives. Photographs of her are now collectors' items and inscribed photographs fetch high sums. London has held a major retrospective of Bernhardt memorabilia fifty years after her death, and two film companies are now making films of her life.

Who *was* this indefatigable Sarah Bernhardt, who had taken as her motto 'Quand même' ('Despite all')?

Débuts and Exits

Sarah Bernhardt's beginning in life was unpromising. That she was born of a Jewish Dutch courtesan, Julie van Hard, and a law student, Edouard Bernhardt, is of little interest and has been frequently recounted. That this liaison in Paris would give life to one of the most romantic figures in history vindicates its repetition. Like many children born into such circumstances the child was sent off to a convent and then to a boarding school for two years and back to another convent. The events that occurred within that framework vary with each narration, perhaps the least plausible account being Sarah's own. Even the exact date of birth is disputed. A birth certificate was not drawn up until 1856 when she was baptised at the age of eleven. Although it records the date as 23 October 1844 other accounts place the day on the 22nd of that month.

Wisely, Julie became the mistress of the Duc de Morny, Napoleon's half-brother who was second only to Napoleon in influence throughout France. It was he who made it possible for the troublesome child to enter the Institut National de Déclamation. It was also he who influenced the academy of the Conservatorie to accept the sixteen-year-old fledgling who had the audacity to début with the childish fable *Les Deux Pigeons*, by La Fontaine. Had it not been for the Duc, Sarah Bernhardt might have had to pursue her career as a nun. Under the tutelage of Provost, who had been Rachel's teacher, Sarah grew in artistic stature until he fell ill and she was forced to study with Samson. He, in spite of his reputation, lacked discrimination in his choice of rôles for his pupils, and Sarah withered in this environment. Discouraged by her experience, she turned again to her mother's lover, the Duc de Morny, who arranged for her to be auditioned by Camille Doucet and Edouard Thierry at the Comédie Française. Given the importance of her patron, it was not surprising that she was accepted, but when she made her début in the part of Iphigénie in Racine's play of that name, her performance was undistinguished. Francisque Sarcey, the French critic, whose opinions on the theatre had been undisputed for forty years, merely noted that she had beauty,

Sarah at the time of her début in *Iphigénie* at the Comedie Française (1862)

Mademoiselle Bernhardt aged 19

poise and articulated well. It was traditional for a young actress to make débuts in three separate plays at the Comédie and in the two which followed that season, Sarah fared no better; Sarcey lamented the low calibre of the entire company. However, he did see in Sarah the germ of an actress, and commented that if she remained at the Comédie Française she might someday attain the level of mediocrity that her colleagues had achieved. Sarah, convinced of her own talent, expected more from the critics, and those who had professed to support her,

15

and on 15 January 1863 put an end to her career at this theatre after a violent altercation with a powerful older actress, Madame Nathalie; she did not wait to be dismissed, but refusing to compromise she stormed into the Thierry's office and destroyed her contract. She felt now that the Comédie could not support her unique talent, and she was prepared to begin again elsewhere.

Once more relying upon connections, Sarah turned to her network of patrons. Her godfather, M. Régis, through the offices of the Director, M. Montigny, was able to obtain an engagement for her at the Gymnase. Making her début there in 1864 at the age of twenty in *La Maison sans enfants* followed by *Le Demon du jeu*, and *Un Mari qui lance sa femme*, Sarah could not have been duller. True, she had grace and good looks, but it was evident to every critic that she had made no artistic progress. All too aware of her shortcomings, Sarah wrote a letter of farewell and apology to Montigny and left for Spain to escape from her failures, saying, with characteristic frivolity that she was off to marry a bullfighter. A more compelling reason for her flight was that she was pregnant, and had no desire to make this known throughout Paris. Sarah had the discretion not to identify the Prince de Ligne, a Belgian nobleman, as the father of her child. She received a telegram summoning her to Paris on the pretext that her mother was seriously ill. Anxiously, she returned to Paris to find she was only slightly ill. When she discovered her daughter's pregnancy, Julie was horrified and found her a separate apartment in the Rue Duphot. It was there on 22 December that Sarah's only son, Maurice, was born. Madame Guérard, a widow who had befriended Sarah in her childhood and was to remain her devoted companion for the rest of her life, took charge of the child while Sarah prepared to return to the stage in April of 1865 as the Princess Desirée in *La Biche au bois* at the Théâtre Porte Saint-Martin. As a stand-in for Debay, Sarah was hardly noticed. In fact, it was the general consensus that her future would be in vaudeville.

Desperation drove Sarah to Camille Doucet, then Director of the Beaux Arts, who introduced her to Duquesnel, joint director of the Odéon. He was captivated by her. A three-year contract in the name of Duquesnel and Chilly was awarded to Sarah, for after all, Doucet was senior to both of these men at the Odéon. All seemed well, but Sarah had been given a choice by the Prince de Ligne: either to marry him or to remain on the stage. It was a difficult decision which caused her much grief. Finally, though she signed the contract.

At first, saddled with a succession of unsuitable rôles in Marivaux plays, she was ignored at the Odéon as she had been at the Comédie.

However, during 1867 she was presented with a wealth of rôles by George Sand, Shakespeare, Molière and Racine. Her Cordelia was splendid, and the voice opened with a sweetness and delicacy that had not before been heard. In Dumas' *Kean* she earned her first personal ovation. Then in 1869, *Le Passant*, by the young poet François Coppée was performed at the Odéon. This was to be Sarah's first unqualified triumph. As the Renaissance page Zanetto, Sarah was a marvel, and this was notable for being the first of many male rôles which she was successfully to play. The excitement her performance caused brought Sarah in this part before the Emperor and Empress in a command performance at the Tuilleries. A succession of minor accolades followed, and Sarah was now a candidate for any major rôle.

Le Passant François Coppée: a shallow, but lovely piece of period nostalgia, in which Silvia, a Venetian courtesan falls in love with Zanetto, a strolling minstrel. Here, Sarah as Zanetto

At this point in her career fate was to intervene: on 15 July 1870 Napoleon III declared war on Prussia. Paris was being evacuated as it seemed certain that the Prussian army would bombard the city. Sarah found a coach for her mother, sisters and son and sent them to Le Havre. She herself stayed behind. As the wounded poured into the city she created her own hospital in the Odéon, and became a nurse in a theatre now housing one-hundred and fifty wounded soldiers. Very little was available to eat and the slight figure of Sarah became more and more emaciated as she gave her food to those who had fought for France.

The signing of an armistice was cause for passionate distress; Sarah's fierce patriotism could not accept the presence of the Prussian army on French soil. She made her way with difficulty to the Hague to be reunited with her family. By March it should have been safe to return to Paris, but the Commune, in its dreadful fury, was taking its toll and did so until the signing of peace with William I, King of Prussia and Emperor of Germany, in May. So not until then could she return to the melancholy and war-scarred capital.

Nevertheless, life in Paris returned swiftly to normal. The Odéon started rehearsing again and Sarah opened in October in *Jean-Marie*, by André Theuriet. As a Breton peasant Sarah was a great success and the play was well received in the battered city. But the great excitement of Paris in the early seventies was the return of Victor Hugo from exile. On 26 January 1872 Hugo's *Ruy Blas* opened at the Odéon. Hugo himself directed Sarah in the part of the Queen and during the rehearsals they had become close friends. On the opening night the brilliant cast included the most important figures of the French stage: La Fontaine, Mélingue, Geoffroy and Sarah. Any doubt of Sarah's power was dispelled that night when the majestic voice rose in Hugo's tragic lines. The audience could not be contained; their greatest poet-dramatist now united with their greatest actress. The play was performed throughout the summer and it was impossible to find a vacant seat for any performance.

Le Passant: A close-up of Sarah as Zanetto

Ruy Blas Victor Hugo: Sarah, as Maria de Neubourg, frail and slender wearing a little crown of silver in her hair

Ruy Blas: The queen has come of age. Sarah in a later revival

New beginnings

As could be anticipated, the Comédie Française from which Sarah had been expelled in 1863 desperately wanted her to return. Emile Perrin was now managing the theatre and he convinced those that mattered that it was time to forgive and forget. Chilly was not about to allow Sarah to default on her contract but he died tragically in June, and Duquesnel allowed Sarah to leave the Odéon.

It is unfortunate that Perrin did not choose more wisely when he picked the play in which Sarah made her second début at the Comédie. After all, at the age of twenty-eight she was no longer an ingénue. *Mademoiselle de Belle-Isle* by Dumas *père* was received with scathing criticism. Sarcey, who had reviewed her Queen ecstatically, pointed out that the costume and powdered hair à la Louis xv ill became her, and that the trembling, convulsive way she spoke her lines was irritating. She was, in fact, a great disappointment. From this point on Sarah would not allow Perrin to choose her rôles, but would carefully select those that suited her, not totally ignoring him, but ensuring that there would be no more failures. There followed a series of minor successes – but not until *Andromaque* of 22 August 1873, was the name Bernhardt again on every lip in Paris. Her regal qualities were both commanding and poignant. Few, if any, of her predecessors had equalled her in this part. Moreover, she was playing opposite Mounet-Sully, with whom she was having a passionate affair, viewed with delight by her public.

Voltaire's *Zaïre* permitted Sarah a brilliant revival in 1874, and many critics were now saying that she was without equal. Perrin listened to them and made an important decision (one that Sarah herself would have made had he not done so): she was to play the part of Racine's Phèdre on the author's anniversary. This was accepted by Parisian audiences as having been Rachel's greatest creation, so it was daring for any other actress to attempt to rival her success. On 21 December 1874

Lithograph by Frederic Regumey of Madame in the rôle of Zaïre in Voltaire's play of that name

Phèdre Racine: Phèdre (to Oenone) 'Why did your wicked mouth dare to accuse and blacken his sweet life?'

Phèdre: (to Oenone) 'Go execrable fiend. Let me command my own poor fate at last.'

Phèdre: (to Oenone) 'Then I shall not see a rival in his heart preferred to me! But anyway your counsels come too late. Oh serve my madness, dear Oenone, not my reason.'

Phèdre: 'I reign? Shall I, shall I make laws of State when my poor reason reigns no more on me?'

Phèdre: (to Oenone) 'By what guile have they deceived me: How did they contrive to meet? Since when: And in what places? You knew all! Why did you let them fool me?'

Phèdre: (Oenone to Phèdre) 'Madame, what are you about? Oh Gods! There's someone coming. You must not be seen. Escape from certain shame.'

Phèdre: 'Ah anguish as yet untried! What more: For what new tortures am I still reserved?'

Sarah's achievement as Phèdre was incomparable. The rôle had now become hers, and she met with the storm of applause that is accorded to the greatest of actresses. She had now established herself to the general theatre-goers of Paris as an actress of great merit and was no longer merely the idol of Parisian students.

Sarah's energy and enthusiasm led her to search for new rôles, but at this time Perrin was warned by her physician that her health was not as sound as she assumed. Possibly she was consumptive. The result was that after the tremendously taxing effort of *Phèdre*, although she was promoted early in 1874 to the position of *sociétaire* of the Comédie Française, Sarah was forced to rest. She found time weighed heavily on her hands, and cast round for ideas to occupy herself. She took up sculpture.

She took a studio near the Place de Clichy where she might pursue painting and sculpture as well as receive at five each day. Her friends became models for her work and a marble bust of her sister Régine was accepted in the Salon of 1875. Inspired by this Sarah took lessons from the sculptor Mathieu Meusnier and in 1896 the Salon accepted a bronze bust and a small plaster cast, entitled *Après la tempête*, which depicted the drowning of some Breton fishermen. In the 1897 Salon she exhibited a bust of Emile de Girardin, the vaudeville writer Busnach, and her friend, the painter Louise Abbéma. Her work was often on a very large scale. *Medea*, for example, was a powerful, life-size work.

A bust of Victorien Sardou by Sarah Bernhardt

Not content with sculpting, Sarah became an art critic as well, and
wrote for *Le Globe*. She also learned to paint and produced a fine like-
ness of herself which was exhibited at the Nouveau Journal. Her unruly
red hair, aquiline nose, closely set intense grey-blue eyes (carefully
lined with kohl) made a compelling subject for a portrait. Her taste for
the macabre (this was the woman who had been known to sleep in a
coffin quilted in rose-coloured silk) produced *La Jeune Fille et la Mort*

Sarah in repose in her
rosewood coffin. Beyond
fulfilling her taste for the
bizarre, the coffin was a
constant reminder of the
transient nature of life. It was
a photograph that she often
presented to close friends

Ophelie by Sarah Bernhardt.
Madelaine Lemaire was the
model

The bronze inkwell

Below left
Sarah the artist with her painting entitled 'Rachel'

Below right
The sculptress with a bust of herself

which was exhibited and engraved for the Salon Folio. A young girl
with the spectre of death looking over her shoulder was bizarre for this
period. But not more so than her later work, *Kiss of the Sea*, which
depicted a girl in the grasp of an immense crab.

She went to the Practical School of Medicine to correct the anatomy
of her portrayals. She visited the dissecting-room and studied the
corpses, prodding them, we are told, with her parasol. She managed to
acquire her own skeleton, called Lazarus. These unusual investigations
resulted in far-fetched newspaper reports of her sadistic experiments at
home decapitating dogs, burning kittens, poisoning monkeys, which
even went so far as to suggest that Lazarus had one time been the victim
of her excesses. The passion with which Sarah pursued her sculpture
and painting was certainly as intense as that which went into her
performances and resulted in the production of forty major pieces.
Perrin lamented to Sarcey, 'I shouldn't mind a *sociétaire* who sculpted
in her free time. What I cannot accept, what distresses me, is that I
have a sculptor who dabbles in the theatre if she has a moment to
spare!'. She entered busts of Georges Clairin and Victorien Sardou in
the 1876 Salon; and they won honourable mention. A self-portrait of
the actress as a sphinx in the form of a bronze inkwell was given to a
few close friends. Another portrait of herself was more enigmatic;
it was a bas-relief in bronze of the Muse crowning Shakespeare and
Molière. It was based upon a published drawing by Clairin in which
Sarah, in a flowing gown, steps forward holding palms in her out-
stretched hands.

Portraits of Sarah executed by Nadar, the Parisian photographer,
show the actress with a terracotta bust of herself and another of her
working on a painting of Rachel. To work she wore white silk trouser
suits and matching shoes designed by herself and Worth, creations
which became the butt of several cutting remarks from critics.

It was during this period that her appartment in Rue Dufour was
burnt down. In spite of her terror of fire she ran in to save her son
Maurice, who was still an infant; everything else was lost, including her
jewel-encrusted tortoise. A benefit performance, starring the singer
Adelaine Patti, was held to help finance the building of an *hôtel* at the
corner of the Avenue de Villiers and Rue Fortuny, large enough to
house all her guests, animals, sculptures and paintings. Félix Escalier
was supposed to be the architect, but characteristically Sarah had much
to do with the final designs and even scrambled up on the scaffolding to
decorate the ceilings of several rooms.

It was at this moment that Dumas *fils* presented the *Comédie* with a
new play, *L'Etrangère* which contained a part specifically designed for

Sarah in the Easter scene of *Gismonda*. Oil on gilt tooled leather

Alphose Mucha's poster for *La Dame aux camélias*

Sarah, that of the Duchesse de Septmonts. But Sarah was not Perrin's favourite, and so when the parts were assigned Croizette, the lady who did hold this honourable position at the time, was given the part, and Perrin even tried to change the title of the play to the *Duchesse de Septmonts*. Dumas resisted this and Sarah made the part of L'Etrangère, Mrs Clarkson, one of her greatest triumphs. *Rome Vaincue* was equally successful and in this, Sarah, rejecting the opportunity of playing an attractive young part asked for the rôle of a blind old woman.

The autumn of 1877 saw the production of Hugo's *Hernani* with Sarah as Doña Sol, and this finally established her position as foremost actress of her time.

La Nuit de Mai Alfred de Musset: In an earlier production Sarah played the Muse and her lover Mounet-Sully played the poet, but here Sarah is the Poet and Julia Bartet the Muse (1909)

Hernani Victor Hugo:
Victor Hugo's favourite
actress

Sarah's position with the Comédie was now becoming strong enough to allow her flamboyance to go unpunished. During the Paris Exhibition of 1878 she was captivated by the idea of a flight in a giant balloon, and persuaded Clairin (who was also one of her lovers) to fly across Paris with her. Crowds of people watched from the ground, as they floated over the Grand Palais sipping champagne. Among the spectators was poor Perrin, whose attempt to fine her for taking an unauthorized journey was quickly overruled by the Ministre des

Paul Berton's lithograph of Sarah as *La Princesse Lointaine*, Melissande

Sarah by Georges Clairin

Beaux-Arts. Sarah was so inspired by her flight that she produced a most charming account of it, seen from the point of view of the chair she sat on, entitled *Dans les nuages: impressions d'une chaise*, and Clairin illustrated it.

Sarah's career with the Comédie went from strength to strength, in

The balloon journey

spite of such difficulties with Perrin. By the spring of 1879 the Queen of Hugo's *Ruy Blas* was the reigning queen of Paris.

A new phase in Sarah's career began with her meeting with William Jarrett, the impresario, who proposed an American tour. However, Perrin and his associates had already planned a season at the Gaiety for 1879 in which Sarah was to participate in a rather minor capacity considering that she was such a renowned actress. Jarrett proposed that the English tour would be more advantageous if she remained an independent *sociétaire* and offered her a contract.

The company arrived at Folkestone, to be greeted by a cheering crowd; that same crowd that demanded that Sarah should be allowed a major part in the London season. As Sarah stepped from the boat an effete young man with long flowing hair stepped forward proferring an armful of lilies which he scattered at her feet. It was Oscar Wilde.

However, when the company arrived at Charing Cross there was no one there to greet them, and to Sarah the city seemed altogether hostile. Gloomily she made her way to the house in Chester Square that had been taken for her. It was there that Jarrett insisted that she see thirty-seven members of the press individually, and it was he who answered all the questions posed; she spoke no English. It became evident to her that if she were to act before foreign audiences she would need just such an agent to inspire her with the necessary confidence.

Her first performance at the Gaiety was nerve-wracking for everyone behind the scenes. In the wings courage failed her, and she was trembling as she walked on the stage as Phèdre. Petite and slender, the fragile figure expressed this fear in a voice pitched much too high, and the performance continued in an almost hysterical tone. The English found this eloquent and poignant: although the ruthless Sarcey proclaimed the performance a failure. Despite this caustic review Sarah was established as London's favourite. Her fear diminished and soon the great full voice poured forth with the same strength and majesty that had conquered Paris. She was fêted everywhere in London society and every door was open to her. Her tremendous will and talent captivated the English. Soon photographs and medallions of her were for sale in all the streets, and Sarah was certain that these were the people who best understood her art. So the London public had won her heart too, and the once gloomy city now offered more pleasure than she had ever known in Paris.

An event, in fact, which was a success almost as great as her London stage performances was the exhibition of her sculpture. She had selected forty pieces to exhibit for sale to the London public in a private gallery. Many were bronzes and paintings executed a few years earlier. It was a spectacular opening for several reasons; it was the first one-woman show seen in London and it was considered unusual for a woman to work in bronze. Sarah, of course, thought of a completely new way of launching her exhibition too – she gave her guests champagne.

Jarrett's proposal of an American tour was still attractive, but Sarah had the experience of Rachel to consider; in 1855 this actress had toured the United States with rather less than success. So although her English tour had gone well, and her exhibition had made a lot of money for her (*Après la tempete* fetching ten thousand francs), Sarah had many doubts about America. When she returned to the Comédie Française, however, the offer was still etched on her mind. On 25 February she gave a splendid performance in *Hernani* and *Ruy Blas* was still a success, but illness and exhaustion together made her a poor Doña Chlorinde in *L'Aventurière*. The resounding boos from the press led her to draft a letter of resignation to Perrin and she sent copies to the newspapers as well. Had she received more letters from Jarrett? No one will know, but Sarah clearly had America firmly in mind.

Jarrett arranged for a contract to be signed between Sarah and Henry Abbey, the American impresario, who was summoned at a moment's notice from America. The tour was to begin the following October. Before this, a second season in London assured her the necessary money to pay the Comédie Française for defaulting on her twenty-year contract, and to build a repertoire to take to America. *Hernani*, *Phèdre*, *Le Sphinx*, *L'Etrangère*, *Froufrou*, and *Adrienne Lecouvreur* (the latter two being completely new additions to her repertoire) were chosen. This was to begin a series of tours of America and the world which would give her a universal stature unheard of in the annals of theatre. Every actor in the French theatre tried to persuade Sarah to cancel that first American tour. They felt she was French and should stay in France. It was to no avail. More determined than ever, Sarah added *La Princesse Georges*, by Dumas *fils*, to her repertoire and *La Dame aux camélias*. This last piece was to be perhaps her most famous and certainly financially her most successful, and yet initially she had her doubts about playing a rôle that for twenty-eight years had been played by many great actresses without success. It was Sarah who brought magic to the play and she was to present it over three thousand times.

Sarah and a cast of seven principals and a handful of supporting actors left for America on 15 October 1880 on the French steamliner *Amérique*. 'Real wealth is the applause of French hands', she had been told by the press. She would decide that question for herself from the other side of the Atlantic.

This undated photograph by Downey of London sums up the grandeur of La Grande Sarah

Adriene Lecouvreur by Scribe
and Legouve: Sarah's version
of this classic legend

Painting by Walter Spindler
of Sarah as Adrienne
Lecouvreur

Adrienne Lecouvreur

A New World to Conquer

On 27 October the *Amérique* ground its way into the ice-bound Hudson river and was greeted by what seemed to be half of America cheering and waving French flags. Overwhelmed by the thousands of admirers who wished to touch her and ask a myriad questions, Sarah staged one of her famous faints into Jarrett's arms. Journalists generated enough publicity to make it unnecessary for Sarah to advertize herself. The civility of the Americans impressed her. Her hotel suite had a salon arranged to resemble her own in Paris, full of fresh flowers, and busts of Victor Hugo, Racine, and Molière. If there were lingering doubts about these people who had rejected Rachel, it was dispelled after her début at Booth's Theatre on 8 November in the rôle of Adrienne Lecouvreur. Her audience called for endless curtain calls and critics on the following day wrote that they had seen 'dramatic genius of the highest order'. Of course there was the conservative element that saw her entire repertoire as risqué, but all of this did more good than harm. Astonishing pamphlets on 'The Loves of Sarah Bernhardt' were sold throughout New York. Her name was exploited in every form of advertising from corset stays to face powders. The American public did not understand her classical repertoire, but responded well to *Frou-Frou*, *Le Sphinx*, *Adrienne Lecouvreur*, and especially *La Dame aux camélias*. On the basis of New York's reactions Sarah modified the repertoire for other cities.

On the way to Boston in the middle of the night Sarah stopped at Menlo Park to visit Thomas Edison. She was already impressed by his

Sarah at the age of thirty-seven

49

Madame in her famous 'bat hat' in 1880

Downey of London posed Sarah in her vampire costume, replete with the bat perched on top of her hat

inventions and wanted to meet the man who apparently even before their first encounter, reminded her of her hero Napoleon. On a bitter night on 5 December Sarah arrived at the estate at Menlo Park which was magically aglow with electric lights. Edison had not gone to see Sarah's New York performances, but welcomed her to his home and laboratory. She was dazzled by his miraculous inventions and breathlessly enquired about them. He asked her to recite something to be

A portrait photograph by Downey of Sarah as Frou-Frou

Frou-Frou by Meilhac and Halévy: The enchanting Gilberte (Frou-Frou) a butterfly caught up in the demi-monde of Paris ignores her child and husband, until she realizes that her sister is taking over her rôle

52

W. & D. DOWNEY
Phot. London

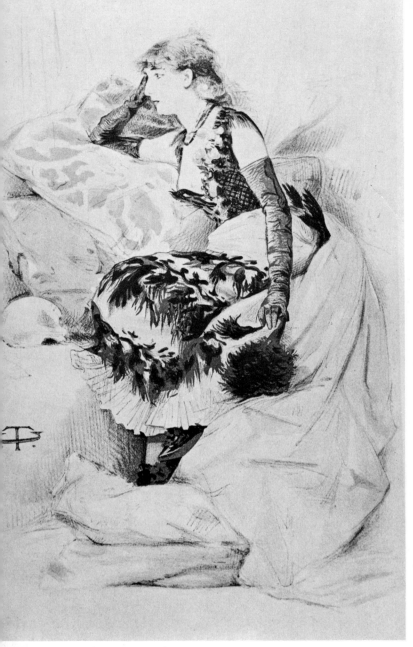

Vanity Fair caricature of
Sarah as Frou-Frou

Frou-Frou: A photograph of
herself in this rôle which
Sarah particularly prized

recorded by his phonograph and she chose extracts from *Phèdre* and *Hernani*. The tinfoil cylinders recorded the voice, and in a few minutes the astonished group listened to her words repeated by a machine. A miracle. The cylinders were never issued, and experts say that if found they would not be playable today. Sarah would later record for posterity, now she had only a few hours to spend with this man she admired so much and then off to Boston for even greater triumphs than those of New York. The Boston Herald proclaimed, 'In the presence of such perfection analysis is impossible'. On to Hartford and Montreal where her performance ended on Christmas Day to endless ovations. Her excommunication by the Bishop of Montreal for performing in *Adrienne Lecouvreur* only amused her, and even more so because it included Scribe, the author of the play who had been dead for some nineteen years. Sarah, smilingly, noted that since the Bishop and she were both in the same profession, they ought to show more consideration for one another. When she arrived in St Louis she found a French-speaking audience that welcomed her so warmly she wished to alter her itinerary and spend three months in this city, but Jarrett reminded her of contracts in Cincinnati and New Orleans. This last city presented an especial problem. The opera singer, Emilie Ambre, just happened to be performing in *La Traviata*, the Verdi opera which uses the libretto of Dumas' *La Dame aux camélias* at the same time as Sarah was presenting the play.

The next day she went on to Mobile. When Sarah saw the size of the stage and the theatre there she was horrified. The only thing to do was to feign illness. It would have been ridiculous to go on. She began to understand the trials of Rachel in this primitive land. She toured through the Middlewest including some of the cities that still have no reputable theatres and encountered many amazing adventures. At one point she ordered the driver of her train to cross the St Louis Bridge at full speed. It had been weakened by floods and was on the verge of collapse. Only when they had crossed and the bridge *had* collapsed minutes after they reached the other side did she realize the possible consequences of her decision. In an attempt at restitution for the risk she had taken with their lives she distributed gold among her cast. She finally arrived in Boston and the cities of the east coast which were infinitely more civilized. In New York she made her farewell on a stage covered with flowers and cheered by well wishers. Although the tour had been trying, she had made a good deal of money and took to heart the pressing requests to return. She was to make eight more American tours ending in that of 1916–18.

Arriving back in Le Havre, Sarah did a spontaneous benefit performance for the coastguards and crowds which had gathered tumultuously to meet her, and then went on to Paris where there was no welcome except from a few old friends. The newspapers proclaimed that her American tour was a disaster and they expressed pity for a woman who had to exploit a country that lacked any discrimination. An attitude of resentment prevailed. Even Sardou had failed her; he had no play to offer, and seemed embarrassed in her presence. Sarah promptly signed a contract for her American touring company to go to London to perform *La Princesse Georges* and *La Dame aux camélias* at the Shaftesbury Theatre. The London public gave her a loving reception and she extended her stay from three to four weeks. The Paris critics were puzzled and enraged. How could Sarah simply desert their theatres? How could London's critics appreciate these performances?

Sarah did not simply return to Paris unarmed; she worked an elaborate strategy in which she contrived, most wickedly, for Madame

La Dame aux camélias: Alexandre Dumas fils: Marguerite believes that she is well enough to see her love. Armand. This is a stage version and not on film

La Dame aux camélias: love's
noble gesture – to leave
Armand

La Dame aux camélias: filming
the party scene

La Dame aux camélias:
Marguerite notes her
consumptive pallor

La Dame aux camélias (on
film: Marguerite, near death
is supported by Armand)

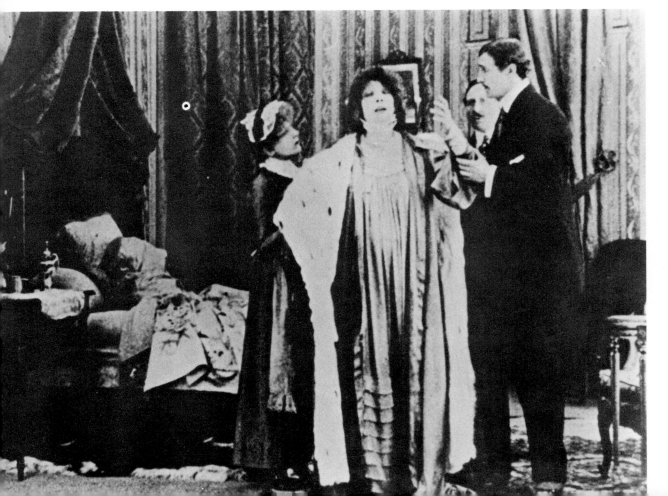

La Dame aux camelias:
Marguerite around 1880

62

Agar to be absent from the Opéra where she was to recite the *Marseillaise* on Bastille Day. About the time Madame Agar was to appear Sarah arrived wrapped in a great cloak and announced that she had already left Paris. The shock was incredible, for the entire diplomatic corps as well as all of the most illustrious members of Paris society were assembled awaiting the majestic ending to the evening. Sarah asked Mounet-Sully to take her cloak, and to everyone's astonishment Sarah was dressed in the classical gown of tragediennes with a tricolour sash! The Paris that had turned against her now had no choice, as the orchestra began to play the *Marseillaise* the whole audience rose to its feet. In a statuesque manner Sarah advanced to the centre of the stage, flag in hand, and paused. The audience gasped an audible 'Sarah Bernhardt', murmured a moment and then in respect for the solemn occasion became quiet. Sarah, in a voice that had not been heard in Paris for a year and a half, intoned the verses of the *Marseillaise* with majesty and then on the last words raised the flag on high and stood motionless. Women wept, men cried out, and the scene was one of wild enthusiasm. Sarah was compelled to recite the entire piece to music three times over. Afterwards the crowd of admirers came to touch her, to kiss the hem of her white gown, and even the newspapers were forced to admit that it was an extraordinary triumph. The devouring monster Paris had been conquered, and she need never fear it again. But she was not immediately to return to a city that did not deserve her. A grand tour of Europe might give Paris some perspective on her art. It was Philippe Garnier, that handsome actor and Sarah's sometime lover who had inspired this project. She had her American tour cast and now Garnier as well. When the news broke the Parisian press and theatre managers were once more astounded. Every persuasion was used to change her mind. Plays were written for her again, theatres were open to her, contracts were ready to be signed. Sarah was amused that those who had scorned her, were now prepared to do anything to keep her in Paris. Her reply was that they should have thought of it before 14 July, then she might have been persuaded by their proposals.

La 'Damala aux Camélias'

It was during the rehearsals for this tour that Sarah's sister Jeanne introduced her to Jacques Damala, a Greek whose real name was Aristide Damala. He was a rogue who had squandered his family's fortune gambling and on the morphine to which he was already hopelessly addicted. His notoriety in Paris was considerable. He was immensely handsome and had apparantly ruined the lives of some very grand Parisian ladies. He told Sarah of his ambitions to become an actor and of his recent appointment to St Petersburg as a member of the French legation. He suggested, with a smile, that she might change her itinerary to include St Petersburg so that she could see him again. Outrageous! She summoned Garnier to suggest a new engagement at St Petersburg, which would entail cancelling ten prior engagements. When he asked for an explanation he was told merely that it would make her very happy to be there. That was reason enough; Garnier had a great affection and devotion for Sarah at this time, and no request seemed too unreasonable.

Sarah's European tour took her from Brussels, Vienna, Odessa, Kiev, St Petersburg, Moscow, Warsaw, Genoa, Basle to Lausanne, Lyons, Trieste and Naples, and everywhere she was received like visiting royalty. She brought back souvenirs of this trip – gems, paintings, exotic animals and all the things that were known to please her. Russia had been an unparalleled success, for the Russian aristocracy spoke French extremely well. She played not only in the theatres of Moscow and St Petersburg (arriving by sleigh) but also at the Winter

Palace of the Czar, and it was Alexander III who bowed before Sarah.

It was no surprise when in St Petersburg Sarah took Damala into her company under the name of Daria. The effect on Garnier was devastating, but, gentleman to the last, he feigned illness and asked to be relieved of his contract in order to return to Paris. There was no bitterness on the part of either Philippe or Sarah. In love she was capable of making disastrous mistakes. Garnier's rôles, and some of those of her other lead actor Angelo, were now assumed by Damala. It was obvious that he was quite incompetent and lacked even the necessary memory to learn all the new rôles. But Sarah's performances still shone, and she was the one the public came to see, for outside Paris the rest of the cast were viewed as little more than stage furniture.

Sarah was determined to marry in spite of the problem that she was Roman Catholic and Damala was Greek Orthodox. But the couple met with constant opposition, until on 4 April 1882, they finally married in London. Although the wedding itself was nothing more than a civil ceremony, the effect on the newspapers was explosive, and the scandal-hungry public throughout the world talked about it incessantly. No one will ever explain the reason for the marriage or Sarah's subsequent undying devotion. It seems that she knew nothing of his addiction to morphine at this stage. Meanwhile she was presenting her fourth season in London. Sarcey was there to acclaim her Doña Clorinde, while Paris seethed at the rebuff. Sarah had no intention of performing before French audiences but she agreed to do a benefit performance at

Bronze medallion struck in Prague, honouring Sarah and Alphonse Mucha. The rôles enumerated are those for which Mucha produced posters

the Gaïté for the widow of the poster artist Cheret, as she was passing through Paris anyway on her way to Switzerland, Spain and Portugal. This would be the first time that Paris would see her in *La Dame aux camélias* and on 25 May 1882, Sarah appeared opposite her husband to a full house which had never witnessed such a production. Three other actresses had played the rôle in the past with only moderate success. Sarah's performance was greeted with enormous enthusiasm, but the critics were scathing about Jacques Damala's 'unfortunate exhibition'. Sarah, however, stalwartly continued to believe in him.

She did return to perform in Paris in July, and was confident that Jacques would be chosen for the part of Loris, the leading man in Sardou's new play, *Fédora*. Sardou was adamant; this was not a part for an aspiring actor. In desperation, because she wanted to open in *Fédora* as soon as possible and because she was equally determined that Damala be given recognition, she went to Catulle Mendès begging for a play explicitly for her husband. Friendship weighed heavily, and he gave her *Les Mères ennemies*, a fine comedy for a strong male lead. Damala was mollified by being told that this was a greater rôle for him, rather than that Sardou had rejected him in *Fédora*. Besides, in this way there would be no competition between them as fuel for the critics. For a small fortune Sarah took the Théâtre de l'Ambigu in the name of her seventeen-year-old son Maurice and made him manager. On 17 November *Les Mères ennemies* opened with Damala and Madame Agar, and to Sarah's relief it was a success of sorts. Now she could open in *Fédora* without fear that Damala would be torn to pieces by the critics.

So for her first real return to Paris for some time, playing opposite the talented Pierre Berton in *Fédora*, Sarah created another masterpiece. The press said that she had surpassed herself, that she was incomparable. Sarah's plan would seem to have succeeded, but Damala felt he had been pushed aside so that he would not enjoy the acclaim that she and Berton were receiving. In a rage he stormed out of their suite in the Avenue de Villiers leaving Sarah brokenhearted. He did not appear for future performances at the Ambigu, and all was apparently at an end. Sarah, could be wounded, but not completely crushed; she returned to *Fédora* with even more vigour and continued anonymously to direct the Ambigu. Upon the closing of *Les Mères ennemies* she selected *La Glu* by the attractive young poet Jean Richepin and employed Réjane and Agar; this apparently distinguished combination did not succeed, and it was followed by two lesser pieces. After ten months of failures Sarah withdrew from the venture at the expense of almost half a million francs. All for love. It was Jean

Fédora Victorien Sarou

Richepin who consoled her and became increasingly close, so much so that the newspapers were busily gossiping of their being inseparable. But by February Damala had returned. He was ill, and Sarah took pity upon him. She promised not to ask for an annulment, but decided that a court separation was necessary when she found that his drug dependence was worsening. He was sent to a hospital for treatment, and Sarah was free to resume her relationship with Jean Richepin.

As soon as *Fédora* ended in April, it became apparent that in order to meet her debts another tour would be necessary. France, Belgium, and the inevitable London. From that point on in her career Sarah rarely missed a season in London. Even when the critics became less generous in their praise, the public still gave her the kind of adoration that she received nowhere else.

Back in Paris Sarah installed herself at the Théâtre Porte Saint-Martin, where she was to give most of her Parisian performances during the following eight years. *Frou-Frou* was revivied to great acclaim and ran for one hundred performances. The culmination of *Frou-Frou* was an even more volatile drama. Unknown to Sarah, during her tour of America in 1880 a member of her company, Marie Colombier, had contracted with a small Parisian newspaper to write a series of articles on Sarah's adventures in America. These were then revised to form a scandalous book thinly disguised under the title *Sarah Barnum*, a title partly used to circumvent the libel laws and partly to evoke the name of P. T. Barnum, an impresario of the grotesque. Sarah's reaction was characteristically explosive. She demanded that the authorities seize all copies. Since they did not comply, she attempted to buy them, but to no avail, as new editions constantly threatened to appear. Sarah, accompanied by her son Maurice, burst into Marie Colombier's house, breaking everything in sight, chasing the culprit from room to room and horsewhipping her.

Frou-Frou was followed by Jean Richepin's *Nana Sahib*. As Djamma, mistress of the Hindu Nana Sahib, Sarah was exotic, voluptuous, and hampered by a most unpoetic script. The critics found it puerile. Marais, who took the part of Nana Sahib, fell ill and the play lumbered on with the author taking over this rôle. Audiences were depressingly small. Early in January of 1884 Sarah surveyed the scant audiences to find Damala seated in the front row looking obviously bored. After his apparent rehabilitation he had appeared with great success in *Le Maître de Forges* by Georges Ohnet. Richepin was outraged by Damala's presence, which had upset Sarah's performance, cornered him at the end of the play and threw him to the ground. Damala, however, continued with several more successes at the Gymnase until audiences finally realized that he was no actor and that he had merely been carried by a series of fine plays.

Sarah soon came to the conclusion that to continue *Nana Sahib* would bring her financial ruin, so she turned once more to standard successful fare. Richepin attempted an adaptation of *Macbeth* for her, but it again was a failure. The relationship seemed doomed on the stage, although Sarah could not have asked for a better friend. Going once more to London Sarah attempted to present *Macbeth* to her adoring London public; but even they could not take it and again *La Dame aux camélias* rescued the season. Upon returning to the Porte Saint-Martin a series of failures plagued her until Derembourg left the directorship and Duquesnel took over the management. Sarah was overjoyed and reassured by this reunion with her first manager at the Odéon. On Sarah's insistence Duquesnel continued to stage *Macbeth* and it fared no better than before. It was not easy to tell Sarah that her love and judgement were confused. Retreating from Paris to Le Havre she began to see things in a more sensible light. If she was going to insist on Richepin's playing the double rôles of lover and leading man, the same ill-fated plays would ruin them both.

Success

Sarah now demanded from Sardou his new play *Théodora* and asked for Phillipe Garnier to be cast as the Emperor Justinian. The events with Damala in St Petersburg seemed to have escaped her memory. Garnier had not forgotten the rebuff, but was both a wise man and a fine actor. He realized that the combination of Sardou and Sarah meant success, and he very much wished to be a part of it. At forty Sarah launched into the rôle of Théodora with all the ferocity this drama demanded. Vulgarity and passion seethed within her as she turned upon the Emperor Justinian, and in the final death scene when the Empress is strangled. (In another version she was led off stage to be garotted, but this was a disappointment for her audience, who liked actually to see her die.) The brilliant acting, sets, costuming and staging marked out this play for immediate success. For an entire year the house was sold out for every performance. The play was taken to London with equal rewards, while in Paris it continued to be performed until Christmas of 1885. Garnier, who was again Sarah's lover, took a strong hand in making decisions; Sarah needed that, and she may also have been making some attempt at reparation for the Damala incident.

After this dazzling success, there followed a difficult period. When Victor Hugo died in 1885 Sarah was genuinely moved. It was this great poet who had given her a diamond tear in gratitude for her welcome for him on his return to Paris from exile, and for her brilliant performances in *Ruy Blas* and *Hernani*. Now she would honour his memory with a

Théodora Victorien Sardou:
The Empress

Théodora: The Empress with
her lover, Andreas (Pierre
Magnier)

Théodora: The Empress fears for the life of her lover, Andreas

Théodora: The Empress Théodora, bars the way to the door so that her lover can escape

Théodora: Fronticepiece for
Sarah's Theatre programme

THÉATRE SARAH-BERNHARDT

Mme SARAH-BERNHARDT   Ph. X

Théodora: The Empress
consoles Andreas (Pierre
Magnier)

Théodora: The assination
attempt, the Empress hears
the name of Andreas called
and bars the door

Théodora: The Emperor Justinian confronts Théodora with accusations

Théodora: The Empress in the Hippodrome tableau wearing one of the most expensive costumes in the history of theatre

THÉODORA

play that he had written in 1831, *Marion Delorme*. With Garnier, Berton, Saverny and Dumaine involved it seemed a certain success. Had not all of Paris turned out for Victor Hugo's funeral and followed behind Sarah who walked the entire route of the funeral cortege? Curiously, the play scarcely lasted a month. The acting was brilliant, but the public found the play dull. Garnier accepted the blame and proposed that Cressonnois and Samson's translation of Shakespeare's *Hamlet* would succeed with Sarah as Ophelia. Unfortunately, he did not fully understand the complex rôle of Hamlet, and in casting himself in this part he failed to please audiences and critics alike.

Everything that had been gained in the production of *Théodora* was quickly lost in these failures and this necessitated reviving *Fédora* and undertaking another tour. This time Sarah planned a fifteen month adventure in South, Central and North America and the whole British Isles. This was to extend from April 1886 to July of 1887. And it was of little surprise that Philippe Garnier should head the company. In South America, Sarah made more money than in any other country –

Marion Delorme Victor Hugo: critical acclaim did not sway the public

Marion Delorme: 'her delivery was magnificent'

in Rio she was given thousands of acres of land in hopes that she might return, while in Brazil, Dom Pedro II, the Emperor, attended every performance. In Montevideo and Buenos Aires, though, her successes were tempered with a great sadness. Jarrett died during the tour and Sarah had to find a replacement for him. Her secretary, Maurice Grau, took his place and was to remain her impressario for the next twenty years. The South American tour ended in Lima, and from here Sarah went to Havana in September and then on to Mexico. Few cities had been as generous as Mexico and Sarah was enchanted with these people and their arts. With sombreros in her trunks she sailed for England. There were no failures, only accolades, jewels, flower-strewn streets, and an income that no person in the theatre had ever earned before.

Sarah had strong misgivings about returning to Paris after her failures there immediately before this tour. Only the magic that she saw in a script presented to her by Sardou in 1887 could convince her to return to the Théâtre Porte Saint-Martin. On 24 November Sarah opened in the third play which he had written for her, *La Tosca* which prompted the remark from one of the first night audience, that the amount of electricity generated in one scene would 'light the streets of London'. It became a rôle Sarah revived and revived, each time sure of a success. Pierre Berton ,now Sarah's 'favourite', was cast in the rôle of Baron Scarpia. This unqualified success played to full houses until 1888 when Sarah became ill from the exhaustion of constant work.

She now turned increasingly to writing. She had begun with *Dans les nuages* after her balloon adventure, and had continued with her critical essays on the theatre for *Le Globe* and numerous miscellaneous articles. *L'Aveu* was her first attempt at playwriting and was performed at the *Odéon* on 27 March 1888. It had been written several years earlier and had been played on tour with much success. Had Sarah performed in it herself at the *Odéon* it might well have been equally popular in Paris, but Raphaele Sisos, who played the leading rôle, could not cope with the pathos of a mother who has lost her child.

In her novel *Petite Idole* Sarah had the opportunity of writing a kind of autobiography in which the heroine an actress, Esperance Darbois, who has a 'golden voice', conquers the hearts of Paris and dies *en scene* – one of Sarah's professed aspirations. Sarah may also have kept a diary, for when in 1906 her autobiography was published it seemed to contain too many details to have been the product of memory. In the last years of her life, Sarah was writing notes which amounted to a second autobiography since her first one ended in the year 1880. These notes were later compiled by her granddaughter Lysiane and published posthumously. At the same time she was writing a work on the art of the theatre. This too was not to see publication in her lifetime but was later published in 1923 under the title *L'Art du théâtre*.

August was spent at her retreat, the old fort on Belle-Isle, a rocky island off the coast of Brittany. With her were Georges Clairin, her faithful companion Madame Guérard, Maurice and his new wife, Terka. This island home was where Sarah would spend almost every summer, except when on tour, relaxing by playing tennis (which she

Nadar

La Tosca Floria Tosca
watches Mario execute a
painting of her in the church
(Act 1)

La Tosca

La Tosca Victorien Sardou:
Madame's first act entry as
Floria Tosca, opera star

always had to win), fishing, shooting game, writing, playing the piano and entertaining the myriad itinerant guests as well as her growing family, all of whom thought nothing of living at Sarah's expense (indeed she herself took it for granted). From 1890 onwards, she initiated the building of many new villas here to house her friends and, areas for her growing menagerie. The cost of this lavish life-style was enormous and she was forced to embark on fresh tours to finance her extravagance. This summer of 1888 was no exception and in September another tour of Europe, Turkey, Egypt, Russia, Sweden and Norway was underway. By the first of March 1889 she was once more in Paris with sounder finances. Here waiting to greet her was Damala, now a spectre, hardly recognizable. Through pity, and perhaps a strange remnant of

La Tosca: Floria contemplates her victim, the evil Baron Scarpia

This famous caricature of Sarah by Léandre appeared in 'Le Rire' in 1889. Sarcey, Victor Hugo, and Sardou look upon the 'Apotheosis of the Grand Tragedienne'. It is said that Sarah's sinuous body established the Art Nouveau curve

love, Sarah took him to a hospital to convalesce for six weeks. Meanwhile she rehearsed *Léna*, which was an adaptation of F. C. Philips' play *As in a Looking Glass*. When it opened on 16 April 1889, with Paul Berton, Damala begged to be present. Sarah brought him to the Théâtre des Variétés and to spare him the brutalities of the press in his present state he was concealed in a screened box. Berton's adaptation was not good and the melodrama was not a success except for its dramatic ending where Léna takes poison and waits for her death. The peculiar triumph of this scene is that for five minutes there is no dialogue. To carry it off certainly required a talent of the magnitude of Sarah's. Damala was especially touched by the scene and expressed a desire to return to the stage with the only woman whom he had ever loved.

The announcement that Sarah and Damala would appear together at the Variétiés in *La Dame aux camélias* brought out all of Paris. But what could be said of a man who was so obviously dying? He could not stand in the final act and yet he continued from mid-May through till July. The burden was becoming too much for Sarah and when she went to London for a season she had to leave him in hospital in Paris. London was treated to *Léna* throughout July and August, and in September a revival of *La Tosca* with Berton at the Porte Saint-Martin brought acclaim, as did her October revival of *Théodora*. On the day of the last performance of *Théodora* Jacques Aristide Damala died. Sarah had never lost her profound love for her husband, despite their separation for so many years. As a tribute she took a bust of him, which she had made herself, to be placed on his tomb at Piraeus.

Léna F. C. Phillips: a silent death of five minutes was unheard of in the French theatre

The Legend

Nothing is more reassuring to an ageing actress than to realize that she still maintains the illusion of youth before her audiences, and at forty-five Sarah chose to play *Jeanne D'Arc* which Barbier had written for her and for which Charles Gounoud had composed a magnificent musical score. Sarah herself staged the production which opened on 3 January 1890. While it was not as successful as Sardou's plays, it was interesting and convincing and enjoyed a fine run of sixteen weeks and then in May was taken to London.

By October it was time to return to Paris with something new. Sardou had presented her with another play *Cléopâtre*. On 23 October 1890 Garnier and Sarah were together again in a most exotic setting. It was the least impressive of all the plays that Sardou had written, but it still had his stamp of genius in those vibrant lines which Sarah, as the languid queen, delivered amidst a set that could well have been her own extravagant salon. Perhaps one of the shortcomings of the play is that it was essentially written for two actors, and the rest of the cast seemed superfluous. This was the last play which Sarah was to perform at the Théâtre Porte Saint-Martin.

At this point she undertook another world tour, perhaps her greatest. It began in New York where in 1891 she presented *La Tosca* to the anticipated ecstatic reviews. The whole of the United States and Canada were included in this grand tour, and then she went on to Australia, Madagascar, Turkey, Constantinople, Athens, Russia, the whole of Europe, North Africa, Dakar, Central America, South

Jeanne d'Arc Barbier: 'a poetic performance'

86

Grasset's poster of Madame as Jeanne d'Arc enjoyed a popularity with the public that was not shared by Sarah; she preferred the eloquent portraits by Mucha

Oil portrait of Sarah by Duane Wakenham, noted California artist

America, Lisbon, and thirty-two months later back to Paris with her company of thirty exhausted actors and actresses. Her repertoire of twenty plays ensured that the critics could not harp on the sameness of her productions.

As soon as Sarah returned in 1893, she took over the management of the Renaissance which unlike the Théâtre Porte Saint-Martin was actually in the theatre district. It was a fine building. This was the first time that Sarah had managed under her own name and she proved to be very astute. Although she concentrated on reviving her famous rôles here, she also produced some very notable new successes. These included *Gismonda*, *Izéil* and *Lorenzaccio*, (in which Sarah took on another of her male rôles, as Lorenzo de Medici), and Rostand's *La*

88

Cléopâtre Victorieu Sardou: This was one of the most widely circulated photographs of Sarah as Cléopâtre. Her tears were almost as famous as her voice

Cléopâtre 'The juice of Egypt's grapes shall moisten these lips no more'

Manuel Orazi's poster for
Théodora depicting Sarah in
the murder scene

Three of Mucha's posters for
Sarah: *La Samaritaine,
Gismonda* and *La Tosca*

Cléopâtre: '. . . that great gap of
time while Anthony is away'

Can the American Woman Design Her Own Clothes?

By Sarah Bernhardt

DECORATION BY
FRANKLIN BOOTH

WHEN I am asked whether, from my knowledge of the American woman, I believe that she can and should design her own clothes I answer emphatically yes, a thousand times yes!

It has always seemed to me a great pity that the countries of the Old World have failed to preserve their original costumes. Of course America, being a new country, did not have such a National costume to preserve; but by reason of this very newness she had a distinct advantage: her women could have created and maintained an individuality in dress if they had not so wrongly adopted, and obstinately clothed themselves according to, French fashions.

The American woman is recognized at once wherever she goes. Her carriage has something independent about it, and she carries herself well. Her small feet—always in movement—show her vital force. Her head, small and delicate and set so well on a long, straight neck, gives a peculiar charm that is characteristic only of the American woman. She is really a being apart in her compelling spirit.

Now I feel that her personality, so absolutely distinct, loses this charm when she doggedly emulates foreign fashions, be they French, Austrian or of other lands. Why should she not be her own distinct self and dress in the style most becoming to her?

Nothing to me is more delightful than a young American woman in her close-fitting American tailor-made suit with its little white collar, topped off with a smart, engaging, appropriate little hat. She is distinctive, attractive, well dressed, and, above all, becomingly gowned.

Again, nothing is more beautiful than the average American woman as she is in the flowing folds of a simple evening dress: she is like a living statue emerging superbly from the graceful drapery that reveals the lines of her figure.

But I ask: Why should this distinctive American figure be ruined, as ruined it is, by the hideous modern corset that is so absolutely unsuited to it?

I stand for the belief that the vitality of the American woman is not yet weakened by the neurasthenia of our Old World women. Her red blood is as yet uncorrupted by the impurities bequeathed to us by our Old World ancestry. The American woman's blood still courses quickly and healthfully through her veins.

Therefore I say that as she is distinctively unlike the Old World woman in all else let her dress herself in her own particular style, direct and simple, and becoming to herself. Then she will have undisputed sway for charm and real elegance.

If she insists that her clothes be made by foreign tailors let it be, at least, by tailors who understand her, and, above all, after her own particular designs, and not after ours. The two styles are absolutely opposed to each other in every respect.

This is my candid opinion and I give it without reservation. It may not please everybody. But, more important than that, let the American woman be American and remain American—in other words, herself.

Sarah Bernhardt

Sarah's syndicated comments on women's fashions from an American magazine of 1910

THE THEATRE

ILLUSTRATED MAGAZINE
OF DRAMATIC AND MUSICAL ART.

Princesse lointaine. Some of her revivals were given a new guise. For instance, the September 1893 production of *La Dame aux camélias* was given a contemporary setting. At this theatre Sarah was successful in launching on their careers several new actors who subsequently became very popular, among them Lucien Guitry and Edouard de Max; and a great coup for her was acquiring the talents of Coquelin *aîné*.

The cover of *The Theatre* in *La Sorcière*, her last success with Sardou

La Princesse Lointaine Edmond Rostand: a popular advertisement for this play

SARAH BERNHARDT.

Théodora: caricture of the Princesse Lointaine

The upkeep of the Renaissance was prodigous, and Sarah's life in Paris was immensely extravagant. In order to pay her commitments Sarah took recourse to her usual way of earning huge revenues – she toured abroad. Her five years of management were interspersed with working visits to all parts of the world, during which time she left the management in the capable hands of Guitry.

On 9 December 1896 it was decided that Sarah Bernhardt was to be fêted for her twenty-nine years on the stage. Five hundred guests assembled in the Grand Hotel, Rue Scribe, to await her entrance. Suddenly all eyes turned to the top of the great spiral staircase where they

Melissande: '... et j'aime la lointaine Princesse'

The gold medal designed by René Lalique for Sarah Bernhardt Day

were greeted with a vision in white, with gold embroidery and chinchilla trimmings. Her descent was accomplished in a series of dramatic episodes, between a series of the velvet-covered pillars around each of which she entwined one arm while gesturing like a queen with the other. A banquet was followed by a chorus singing her praises, and a gold medal with Sarah's profile in relief designed by René Lalique was presented to Sarah and a fortunate few. With a consummate sense of timing she ascended the stairs again, like a baroque assumption, and disappeared. Later these same guests appeared at the Renaissance to see Sarah in the fourth act of *Rome Vaincue* and the third act of *Phèdre*. Finally the curtains opened again upon Sarah enthroned as Phèdre and all her poets and dramatists read their poems of homage while thousands of camellias were tossed upon the stage. Sarah was now an institution. She had gone so far beyond every actress in the history of the French stage that comparisons were inappropriate. It seems ironic that after this great tribute, her final two years with the Renaissance saw little but a succession of financial failures, saved at the last moment by revivals of old favourites, and very occasionally by a new success such as Rostand's *La Samaritaine*.

Comparisons have been made between Sarah and a number of other actresses, in particular Eleanora Duse. These comparisons are meaningless, for as actresses they were completely different. Sarah was great in the classical tradition and above all a brilliant tragedienne who was at home with the works of Corneille and Sophocles but equally with the tragic heroines of Sardou. La Duse did not, and could not have played these rôles with conviction; limitation, not choice, left her with a repertoire of melodrama in which her understated artistry was superb. The ill-fated competition between Bernhardt and Duse was maliciously contrived by Gabriele d'Annunzio to whom Duse was slavishly devoted. It was after all the generosity of Sarah, who made her Renaissance Theatre available to Eleanora Duse without charge, that permitted the Parisian public to ever see this most famous Italian actress. D'Annunzio had contrived for Duse to play two of Sarah's greatest rôles, *La Femme de Claude* and *La Dame aux camélias* (the latter having been in Sarah's repertoire for sixteen years). The plot was obvious, but the provocation ensured audiences for the ten nights for which she was scheduled to appear, and the reaction of the public was favourable, although the critics found La Duse's Marguerite too middle-class in conception. Yes, she had lived up to her reputation, but in no way could she eclipse the vivacity, pathos and ardent love encompassed in the performance of La Grande Sarah.

On 14 June 1897 Eleanora Duse and Sarah performed together at the Renaissance in a benefit performance in honour of Alexandre Dumas *fils*. D'Annunzio was present in the audience, for he had heard of the preference of the French public and critics for Sarah. He had anticipated the very opposite reaction. The consequence of this was tragic. D'Annunzio berated La Duse for playing against Sarah and expressed his admiration for the genius of the great Bernhardt. Further he declared that his next play would be written for Sarah. The duel ended in the great sorrow that was to permeate the life of La Duse and cause her premature retirement at the age of fifty. D'Annunzio kept his promise and wrote *La Città Morta* for Sarah. She accepted it, in spite of its poor quality, perhaps because he was attractive, famous and young. D'Annunzio did not understand the French public, and the topic of incest did not endear him or the play to them. The play scored a record new low of thirteen performances in 1898.

The season of 1897 opened on 15 December amidst all the clamour in Paris surrounding the Dreyfus case. Sarah had pronounced his innocence from the very beginning, despite the fact that this alienated her from her son and many figures in the theatre. It was she who exhorted Emile Zola to write his 'J'accuse . . .' in support of Dreyfus in *Le Figaro*. Sarah was appearing at this moment in a controversial play by Mirabeau entitled *Les Mauvais Bergers* and the audience came as much to hear her political views as to see the play. Sarah had partisans in the audience cheering and booing various lines. It was

La Samaritaine Edmond
Rostand: Sarah as Photine

La Samaritaine Photine at the
well, Mucha's inspiration

chaos. When the public marched on Zola's house and demanded his head for supporting Dreyfus, it was Sarah who appeared at a balcony window; the mob was stunned and dispersed. Soon demonstrations against her were staged around the Renaissance and Mirabeau's play was interrupted. Sarah firmly stood by her convictions.

After this political episode, Sarah encountered more and more difficulties with the Renaissance. Failure after failure led her to the conclusion that the theatre was ill-fated, and so after a farewell performance of *La Dame aux camélias* on 11 December 1898, she abandoned it and wrote off the two million francs she had lost over it. The farewell was not too sad, though, because the Municipal Council of Paris had agreed to lease her the Théâtre des Nations for twenty-five years, the contract to take effect on 1 January 1899.

Théâtre Sarah Bernhardt

Some said that Sarah took the larger theatre because it would enable her to keep a greater distance from the audience and thus preserve the illusion of youth. Sarah was at this time fifty-five years of age, and strikingly handsome. What nature had effaced was little, and that could be changed with a bit of kohl and rouge. It was in this theatre, now renamed the Théâtre Sarah Bernhardt, that she was to perform for the last twenty-three years of her life under the management of Victor Ullmann and her son Maurice. During the first fifteen years in this new theatre she served as manager, producer, star, and occasionally, writer. Age and illness finally made it necessary for her to allow others to worry about receipts.

La Tosca was chosen to open Sarah's grand theatre on 21 January 1899. Pierre Magnier played Mario and André Calmettes was seen as Scarpia. Sarah felt a new freedom of movement on this large stage. She was a petite woman barely over five feet in height. Her entrances, especially before a new audience, betrayed a tiny figure with a disappointingly thin voice. However, flower-like she would unfold as the play progressed, the gestures becoming ever more expansive and the voice swelling to the grand crescendoes that had made her justly famous. This combination produced the impression that she filled even the large stage of her new theatre. It was this impression, La Grande Sarah, which Mucha depicted in his elongated posters, rather than the diminutive reality. By the end of three hundred performances the receipts allowed for experiment. Sarah decided on the unfortunate revival of a previous failure, Feuillet's *Dalila*. The cavernous theatre remained almost empty, and after two weeks Sarah wisely withdrew the production and five days later appeared in *La Samaritaine*. In April *La Dame aux camélias* was revived, as it would be each time receipts fell. Sarah's penchant for plays that the public would not enjoy necessitated its frequent performance.

One great obsession of Sarah was to play *Hamlet;* not the unrewarding rôle of Ophelia, she had already done that, but the character of Hamlet himself intrigued her as had the rôle of Lorenzo de Medici. No existing French version of *Hamlet* appealed to her. She felt the lines were quite unnatural, so Eugène Morand and Marcel Schwob were commissioned to rewrite Shakespeare for her. On 20 May 1899 Sarah opened as the melancholy Prince. Her performance was completely unlike any seen previously in Paris.

Hamlet: Shakespeare's text adapted by Marcel Schwob, Eugene Morand, Lucien Cressenois and Charles Samson: The graveyard scene

Hamlet: 'Princess of Denmark'

Hamlet: the same scene in
another production

The Comédie Française version with Mounet-Sully might have been a different play. There was as much controversy over the interpretation as over the fact that Sarah was once more in the dress of a man, but nevertheless it was an undeniable success. As Hamlet bent on revenge, Sarah moved about the stage panther-like with the vitality of a young man. When Sarah left for London in June it was to take Shakespeare back to the English at the same time to allow alterations to be made to her theatre. Clement Scott, and English critic, found Sarah 'imaginative, electrical, and poetical', and Maurice Baring said that at last the French had found out what *Hamlet* was all about through the artistry of Sarah Bernhardt.

Usually Sarah would return to relax at Belle-Isle, but now it was necessary to supervise the remodelling of her theatre. Her three friends Alphonse Mucha, Georges Clairin, and Louise Abbéma were commissioned to paint ten enormous murals of Sarah in her greatest rôles: *Lorenzaccio*, *Gismonda*, *Phèdre*, *Théodora*, *La Princesse Lointaine*, and *La Tosca*. The rest of the interior was draped in a yellow velvet. No actress had ever before enjoyed a dressing room consisting of a suite of

Hamlet: addressed by Polonius, 'What do you read M'Lord' 'Words, words, words...'

Hamlet: The 'duel scene' from the Paris Exhibition film of 1900

five rooms on two levels which included a grand salon and a dining room with its own kitchen.

Hamlet was brought back to this gloriously appointed theatre and played for three months to packed houses.

At the Paris Exhibition of 1900 a 'moving picture' of Sarah Bernhardt and Pierre Magnier (as Laertes) in the duel scene from *Hamlet* was shown in the Phono-Cinéma-Théâtre. This was one of the very earliest films. Fortunately a few yards of it are still in existence, but the sound transcription supervised by Clément Maurice and recorded on cylinders is lost. Sarah rarely spoke of the film, but it was to mark the transition of a great stage actress to the more permanent medium of the cinema.

Rostand, who was rapidly becoming France's foremost poet, late in 1899 presented Sarah with the manuscript of a new play, *L'Aiglon*. With considerable persuasion he was brought to Sarah's new theatre to read the entire manuscript to her company. He was ill and it was an effort for him to come from his home in Cambo to Paris, but at Sarah's command he came. The reading was an immense success. The cast wept and applauded. On the opening night of 15 May 1900 *L'Aiglon* proved to be all that Rostand and Sarah had hoped for. As the Duc de Reichstadt on the plain of Wagram, Sarah achieved one of her greatest triumphs, and the death scene, which took place before the cradle in which she (the Duc) was born, the audience sobbed. Thirty curtain calls greeted Sarah and the audience screamed for Rostand. From this point on Sarah would be as closely identified with this rôle as with *Phèdre* and *La Dame aux camélias*. The play ran through October, and Sarah made as much money from this run of *L'Aiglon* as she had lost in five years at the Renaissance.

Lest America should forget her, Sarah planned, with Maurice Grau, a return visit with Coquelin as Flambeau in *L'Aiglon* and as Scarpia in *La Tosca*. In *Cyrano de Bergerac* Maurice waggishly asked if Sarah was going to play the part of Cyrano, a prophetic joke, because indeed in 1909 she did. It was a happy combination that opened at the Garden Theatre in New York on 26 November 1900. *Cyrano*, *Hamlet*, *La Tosca*, *L'Aiglon* and *La Dame aux camélias* were played in most of the large cities of the United States. In April the company appeared once more in New York to play *L'Aiglon* for two weeks in the Metropolitan Opera House.

Returning from the United States for a London season Sarah calculated her time so that she might be in Paris with *L'Aiglon* for Bastille day. On 14 July 1901 Sarah gave one of those magical performances of which she was able to say '*Dieu était là*'.

L'Aiglon Edmond Rostand: Franz thinks upon his father's works, 'He would but ape me, if he made great wars –'

L'Aiglon: The Duke woos his grandfather, the Emperor

L'Aiglon: Thérèse tells the Duke of his origins in a divine race

L'Aiglon (on the plain of Wagram): The Duke, Franz, thinks upon his father, 'My son shall reign – a mighty sovereign'

L'Aiglon: the Duke, 'You can only hate me, for I am Wagram manifest before your eyes'. The Emperor, 'Out of my sight! Begone!'

Lacroix
phot

L'Aiglon: Franz, 'To battle in
this tumult you commanded!
Oh Father – Father—'

L'Aiglon: the Countess, 'He
snatches at the cradle's lace,
as if to make a winding sheet'.
Franz, 'I must remember how
they christen better in Paris
than they bury in Vienna.
General Hartman!'

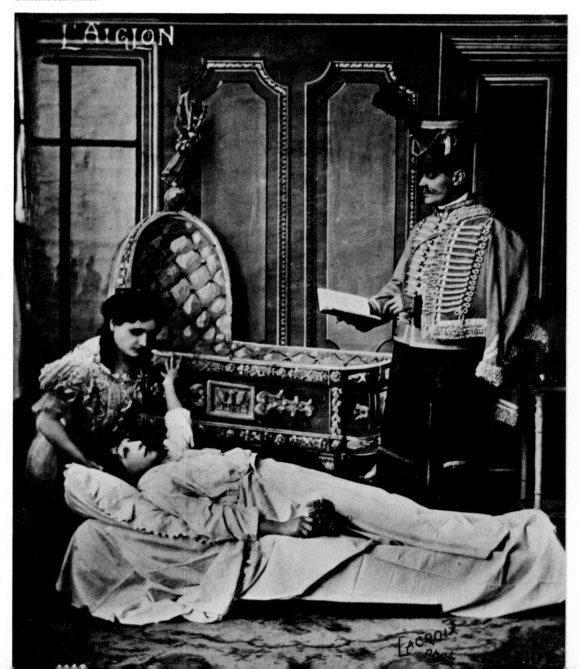

P. BOYER
Phot.

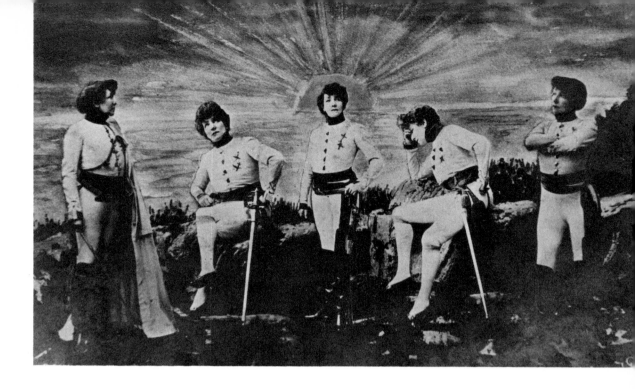

L'Aiglon: a montage of Franz, Duke of Reichstadt, upon the plain of Wagram

L'Aiglon: Franz, '. . . Renouncing, praying, asking to suffer . . .'

L'Aiglon (on the plain of Wagram): Franz, 'Like an impatient lover I've come too early to my tryst with France.'

L'Aiglon: Franz, 'It were like kissing France upon the lip if Paris took me to her breast'

L'Aiglon: the Duke, in pensive mood, murmurs, 'Complete my work, and not avenge my death – all patriots'

L'Aiglon: Franz, 'The lies they've told me make the truth more dear, Oh Freedom, Freedom, thou hast nought to fear from one so late unfettered'

Cyrano de Bergerac Edmond Rostand: 'an incredible triumph' as Roxane

Cyrano de Bergerac Sarah playfully reversed rôles and played Cyrano

Madame and Coquelin *ainé*, co-stars of *Cyrano de Bergerac*

Cyrano de Bergerac: The haughty, Roxane

In 1902 Sarah performed for the first time in Germany in *Fédora*. She had not forgotten 1870 and they had not forgotten her arrogance in avoiding them on all her world tours. (She had been asked frequently to perform in various parts of Germany but each time her fee had been too great – she had requested Alsace-Lorraine.) When she finally appeared, she was received with mixed emotions by the audience, but she did fill the houses. *Simplissimus*, a cartoon journal, depicted a Sarah before a French audience with a flag reading 'Vive la France' and the same Sarah before Germans with 'Deutschland über alles' as her motto. But Sarah's allegiance was beyond question. Wilhelm II gave a luncheon for her in Potsdam which nearly ended in a diplomatic

incident. A toast was proposed to the French artists and Sarah amended it to 'The whole of France !' The room went silent.

The Théâtre Sarah Bernhardt was not markedly successful during 1902 to 1903 but in December of 1903 Sarah scored a great success with a new play by Sardou (destined to be his last), *La Sorcière* was to have numerous performances in Paris and on tour. The play ran on well into 1904 and was the hit of that season. Sarah had a strong personal interest in the occult. This fascination had been the reason for her accepting the rather inferior play *Spiritisme*, which had been among her failures at the Renaissance some years before. She was known to have participated in séances and occult phenomena had deeply influenced her friends Sardou and Mucha. *Théroigne de Méricourt* which followed was a grand production but lacked vitality. It did not survive the year. Only Sarah's confidence kept it on the stage even for this brief period.

The Recording Artist

During an early tour in New York Sarah had visited the Gianni Bettini Phonography Laboratory on Fifth Avenue and cut a cylinder of a dramatic passage from *Izéil* as well as 'Un peu de musique' from Victor Hugo's *La Légende des siècles*. There is no evidence that these original recordings on five inch wax cylinders have survived. Certainly they were not listed in the Bettini catalogue of 1898. The cylinders were fragile but gave fine quality with little surface noise. The Phonoscope praised the 'excellent reproduction of the actress's impassioned delivery'. Sarah listened to the recordings and approved of them and one of Bettini's favourite photographs was that of Sarah delightedly listening to a playback of her own voice.

Pathé cylinders in 1902 was already a well established firm in Paris and they were eager to capture the 'golden voice' on fifty-five millimetre and ninety millimetre cylinders. Racine, Musset, Hugo and Sarah's son Maurice were the dramatists she chose to record. Victor Hugo's 'La Chanson d'Evirandnus' was a poem recounting adventuresome lovers in the spring of their love. Her voice evoked forest birds, flying steeds and the mysteries of a youthful love. This, and *La Fiancée du timbalier* were well known in France and were certain to sell, as of course was *Phèdre*. A passage from Musset's *Lucie* fared less well, and *Le Lac* by Maurice Bernhardt was a feeble piece and was probably written by Henri Cain who assisted him in most of his later literary attempts. These cylinders were released in 1903 and well received by the public and critics. In *Phèdre* they noted the tremulous 'E string of

Sarah appears in the lobby of her theatre before the premier of *Varennes*. With her are the authors of the drama, M. Lenôtre and M. Lavedan

124

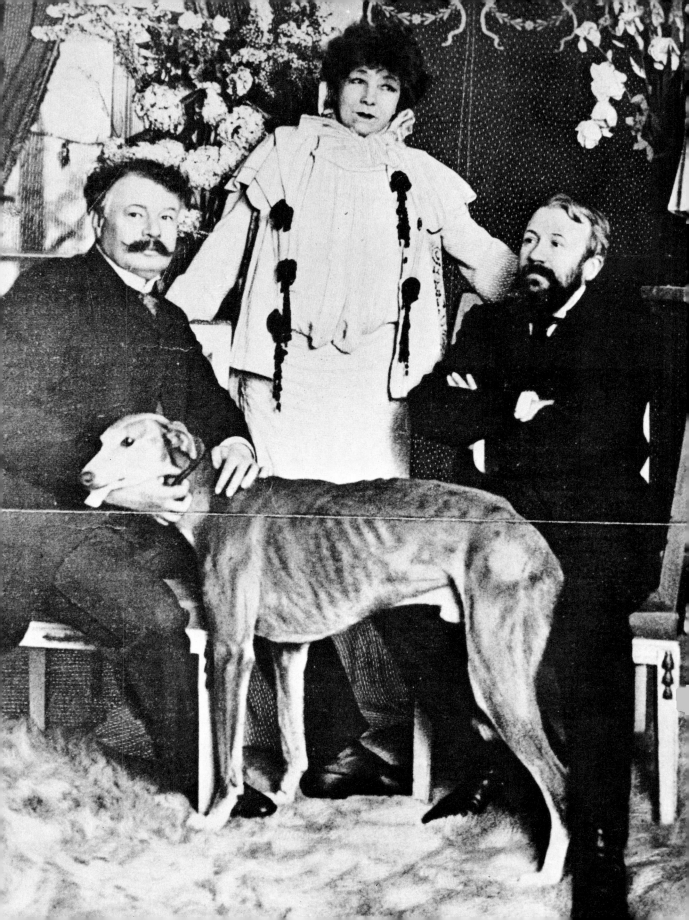

her throat'. As to the character of this voice it might be classified as an extremely versatile dramatic soprano. Certainly it was large enough to resound in her own theatre and to fill the Roman theatre in Orange where she gave performances in July of 1903. Lytton Strachey said upon her death, '. . . there was more than gold, there was thunder and lightning, there was heaven and hell'. The recordings, however, have been more faithful to the upper register than to the lower.

In 1903, too, the Paris Gramophone and Typewriter Company recorded six discs bearing the hallmark 'Black G and T Discs'. Once more she recorded Maurice's *Le Lac*, and another piece that he had written for her, *La Mort d'Izéil* (not from the play of that name). Copée's *Un Evangile* enjoyed a considerable popularity, but even more interest was elicited in *La Samaritaine* and this preserves some of Sarah's best recitation. In deference to Rostand, Sarah also recorded a piece written by his wife, Rosemonde Gérard, *Les Vieux*. Sarah would always compromise an aesthetic ideal to favour a friend. All of these have survived with the exception of *La Mort d'Izéil*, which one hopes will surface someday.

Listening to transcriptions of these discs, one has the impression that little, if any, progress had been made in the technique of disc recording. The surface noise was even more pronounced than that of the earlier wax cylinders. The life expectancy of the disc, however, seemed generally greater.

In the same year the Zonophone company of Paris recorded the dream sequence from Paul Hervieu's *Théroigne de Méricourt* as well as making a third recording of *Un Peu de musique* by Victor Hugo. The former piece reveals a low-key, ethereal, trilled chant that gives it a luminous quality. It is interesting to note that in her recordings Sarah trilled her 'r's in order to achieve a musical vibrato, although this was not part of her stage technique; it was this form of dramatic declamation that was taught in the Conservatoire of Paris established in 1786. When the *chant* itself was replaced by *vérité* this meant little more than a change of emphasis from recitative to a conversational style based upon text. While never subscribing to *vérité* in recorded performance or on stage, Sarah became influential in vitalizing and liberating the word within the context of formal poetry and prose. Were it not for this, she could never have mesmerized American audiences who understood nothing more of spoken French than was to be read in the programme synopses. The greatest of all instruments, the human voice, was being played by the most vital imagination of the time.

Tragedy

The Théâtre Sarah Bernhardt was now so well established that Sarah was able to leave on tour and have others perform her rôles without a loss of revenue. The year 1903 saw several minor failures, but Sardou's *La Sorcière*, *Gismonda* and *Cléopâtre* were successes enough for any theatre season.

Varennes, in which Sarah played Marie Antoinette, opened the season on 23 April 1904. Although Sarah was radiant, Lavedan and Lenôtre were perhaps too historical and the play ran only until June. However, this was her usual London touring season and she left with *La Sorcière* which proved a great hit in London. In 1905 Sarah created Tisbé in Hugo's *Angelo, Tyran de Padoue*, with Desjardins and De Max. The opening on 7 February was greeted with much acclaim. Easter saw a revival of Racine's *Esther* in the manner in which it was first presented at the Ecole de Saint-Cyr. The public was puzzled by the staging and this lack of comprehension did not establish the work as a success.

In April of 1905 Sarah left for London where she played *Pelléas et Mélisande* with Mrs Patrick Campbell. These two actresses were tremendous friends and continued to rely on one another and correspond throughout their lives. They both had an excellent sense of humour, and it was during one of the performances of *Pelléas* that Sarah gently took Mrs Patrick Campbell's hand and squeezed a raw egg into it. The two continued the scene barely able to conceal their mirth. Equally close a friend was that other remarkable actress Ellen Terry, who paved the way socially for Sarah whenever she came to

La Sorcière: Zoraya goes to the stake before a howling mob

La Sorcière: Zoraya protests her innocence before Ximenes

La Sorcière Victorien Sardou: Zoraya, the beautiful Moor

Varennes: Sarah, with Maurice, in the rôle of Marie Antoinette

Angelo Tyran de Padoue:
Victor Hugo: A beautiful and
formidable Tisbe. Madame
at sixty-one

Esther Racine: In the rôle of
Assuerus in Racine's late
tragedy Sarah was splendid
but played to an
unappreciative audience in her
own theatre (1904)

Angelo Tyran de Padoue
Tisbe receives council

Pelléas et Mélisande Maurice Maeterlinck: Madame as Pélleas and Mrs Patrick Campbell as Mélisande in a London performance of the play (1905)

London, and was always most generous in her public praise of Sarah's Art. June saw the beginning of another tour of the Americas, the great draw of which was to be Sarah's own version of *Adrienne Lecouvreur*, a substitute for Scribe and Legouve's play which she had performed, with great reluctance, for twenty-five years.

Esther: Sarah in the same rôle

133

In October the company was in Rio de Janeiro where a tragedy occurred. Here Sarah performed *La Tosca* on the ninth of that month. As La Tosca leaps to her death from a parapet of Saint Angelo Castle a mattress below breaks her fall. This time it was not there. In agony Sarah refused to allow any doctors to help her. The one who did come to see her was so dirty that even though her cast promised to bath him, she would not consult him. She had fallen on that leg as a child and again at school. Sarah insisted on sailing to New York where she would find a doctor to her liking. It was a painful trip of three weeks. The

André Gill's famous rendering of the fluttering Sarah

New York season was postponed for two further weeks while doctors worked on her leg with little success. By the middle of November she walked haltingly and decided to proceed with the Chicago engagement. The injury had not healed, and it was apparent to the audience that Sarah was in pain. This pain would never leave her. Ether was rubbed on the leg, and those hateful shots of morphine had to be administered when walking became impossible.

The newspapers reported this incident and announced that it would be Sarah's last visit to America. In sixty-two cities the auditoriums and theatres (or tents) were filled to capacity. When the draw was so great that other performers were getting no audiences, managers in the West refused to back her. Whereupon, undaunted, she had a huge tent erected and taken from city to city in the West. Financially the trip was a great success. Sarah even learned to make money playing poker with friends on the train; of course they were obliged to play by her rules, as she leaned across the table, gathering up everyone's chips, saying beguilingly 'cheeps, cheeps'.

Upon returning to France, Sarah immediately left for London for a three week engagement, but wracked with pain and fatigue she soon returned to Belle-Isle and it was now that she wrote most of the autobiography *Ma Double Vie*, her memoirs from birth to the year 1880. A secretary wrote everything down as Sarah dictated it. She was more interested in style than accuracy, and as a result the book was a great success in France and translated into English.

La Vierge d'Avila was finally ready for the stage in November of 1906, after much argument between Sarah and Catulle Mendès, the author. One may speculate that after all the correspondence Sarah might well have been credited as co-author. Opening on the tenth of that month Sarah mustered up all of the passion of her youth in the Grand-Champs convent to play 'God's coquette', Saint Theresa of Avila – another death scene, and another triumph for Sarah and Catulle Mendès. Jean Richepin and Henri Cain had together written *La Belle au Bois-Dormant*, an adaptation from Perrault's fairy tale. As Prince Charming the sixty-three year old Sarah was the image of a handsome adolescent. . .

The season of 1908 to 1909 brought Sarah so much pain that it was very difficult to walk. Productions had to be restaged so that she could lean on props or be seated, but *La Dame aux camélias*, *La Tosca*, *La Samaritaine* and *La Sorcière* were all successful as ever. In May she played the young poet in *La Nuit de Mai* by Musset opposite Adeline Dudlay in her farewell performance in the Rue de Richelieu. November saw the mounting of a new production, Emile Moreau's *Le Procès de*

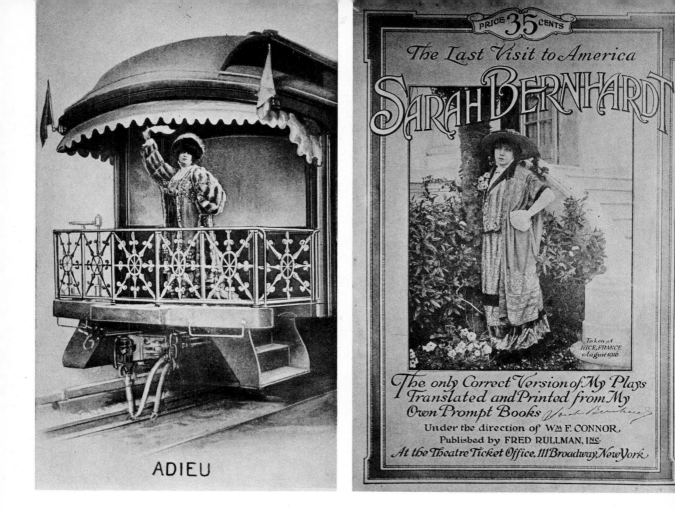

ADIEU

The Last Visit to America

SARAH BERNHARDT

Taken at
NICE, FRANCE
August 1916

The only Correct Version of My Plays
Translated and Printed from My
Own Prompt Books
Under the direction of Wᴹ F. CONNOR,
Published by FRED RULLMAN, Iɴᴄ.
At the Theatre Ticket Office, 111 Broadway, New York

Jeanne d'Arc. When asked her age, the maid of Orleans slowly turned facing the audience and in the voice of a girl replied 'nineteen'. This gesture was bold enough to bring thunderous applause.

Success encouraged Sarah and she produced her own play *Un Coeur d'homme* on 22 December. This four act drama was played by Blanche Dufrène and Emmy Lynn. Sarah directed a play in which she ought to have starred. It was not a commercial success, nonetheless she did not cease to believe in it, and had it published in one volume along with her play *L'Holocauste* in 1911.

The 23 of October marked her departure for America on a 'farewell tour'. In the cast of thirty was a young man Lou Tellegen, a former model of Rodin, aged twenty-seven, who would be Sarah's leading man for the next three years in Paris, London, and on the tours of 1910–11 and 1912–13. Tellegen was not a great actor, but his youth, good looks, and devotion naturally endeared him to Sarah. On 10 November Sarah

The final photograph in Sarah's official Farewell Tour Souvenir Programme

A programme from one of Sarah's four 'Farewell Tours of America'

La Vièrge d'Avila: Catulle Mendes: Saint Theresa

137

This framed photograph of Sarah in *Une Nuit de Noël* was presented to her in 1913 by the prisoners of San Quentin as a gesture commemorating her free performance of 22 December

Sarah performing *Une Nuit de Noël* at San Quentin. The prisoners printed a programme for the performance

A touching moment in San Quentin when Sarah is thanked for her generous gesture.

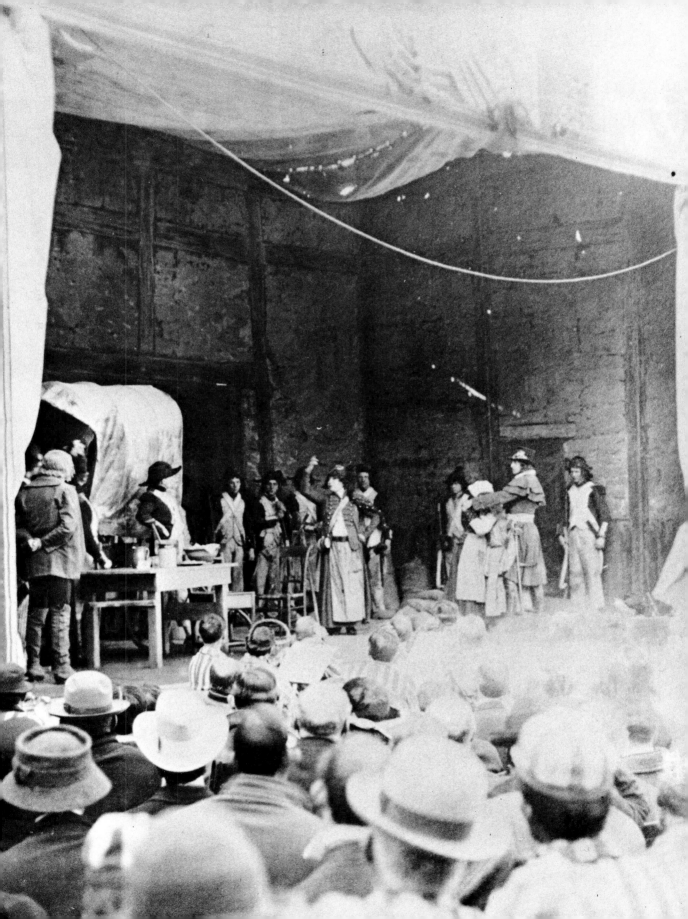

opened in Chicago with great success and by the time she was in New York she had added a new rôle to her repertoire, *La Femme* X by Alexandre Bisson and followed in two weeks with another new play *Judas* by the American John De Kay. As Judas she gave only one performance. The rôle did not appeal to her, it was done as a favour though it demonstrated her continuing versatility. In February of 1911 she played before two thousand prisoners in San Quentin Prison. They stood to applaud her in *Une Nuit de Noël sous la terreur*. Fearlessly she took a ride in an open two seated plane to the delight of cheering prisoners.

Les Bouffons: Miguel Zamacois: Jacasse, the eloquent bouffon

La Beffa Sem Benelli: The ironical Gianetto Malespine delighted Sarah and not her public

At this time further effort was put into new recordings. Sarah was informed that Pathé had a new kind of recording which they called the 'etched-label disc', and she was invited to commit her art to posterity once more. *Les Bouffons* by Miguel Zamacois had brought her some success. The monologue 'La Legende du Zephyr' from this was recorded but never released. Fortunately, Sarah re-recorded it in 1909 at the persuasion of Thomas Graf, one of Edison's representatives abroad. In addition to these she duplicated her recitations on discs for the same firm, including 'La Tirade du nez' from Rostand's *Cyrano de Bergerac*. A recording of another declamation from *Phèdre* reinforced the already increasing releases of this work which had become quite popular in America as well as Europe. The first tableau from *La Samaritaine*, intended as a dialogue between Photine and Jesus, became something of a monologue when Sarah decided that Jesus's lines had to be cut severely. This disc reveals the melodic quality of the Bernhardt voice in an enchanting lullaby. Outstanding among these four-minute Amberol cylinders released from West Orange, New Jersey, was the great Wagram scene from *L'Aiglon* – perhaps the finest recording Sarah ever made. Sarah once said of her partner Mounet-Sully 'His voice was an orchestra of sound'; the same may be said of her in this moving monologue. The musical nuance, the sense of time and the sustained control of the poetic line are remarkable.

Immortality

Since her first formal portrait by Nadar in 1863 Sarah had been photographed by Boyer, Sarony, Downey, Manuel, and every significant portrait artist of her time. The accumulated photographs, she maintained, would, if stacked, be as tall as the Eiffel Tower. This sort of immortality was not enough for her when there was a new medium to be conquered. There was a period between 1909 and 1918 when Sarah concentrated on establishing herself as the first motion picture star, and neglected recording totally. Her oft-quoted aversion to film-making is to be taken lightly, for there is much evidence to the contrary. Sarah said of the motion picture industry 'it exorcized the old curse on the actor's art – it's impermanence'. Although she was appalled by most of the films that she had seen in the first decade of the twentieth century and referred to them as 'those absurd photographic pantomimes', she knew she could do better, and viewed the medium as 'my last chance at immortality'.

So in 1908, Sarah went with her cast to the market place at Belleville to film *La Tosca*. The results did not please her, and she asked that it should not be released. Lucien Guitry, Paul Mounet and Edouard de Max had all been taken on location with Sarah and the director André Calmettes. How could the film have failed? Blaisdell writing in 'Moving Picture World' said that in 1911 *La Tosca* was released under the auspices of Film d'Arte and Universal Features with a cast of de Max, Denenbourg (Cavaradossi) and Maury (Angelotti). No mention is made of the renowned figures of Lucien Guitry or Paul Mounet. This two reel film of forty minutes Blaisdell found 'gripping' as well as having 'fast action'. He notes further that the film was retracted upon the death of Sardou. Were there two *La Toscas*? Were both filmed in 1908?

In spite of the fact she was not pleased with *La Tosca*, by 1911 Sarah had already decided to film a part of her famous stage success *La Dame aux camélias*. For thirty years she had electrified audiences as Marguerite Gautier and now she was determined to make a permanent record of her performance, beginning with Marguerite's separation from Armand (played by Lou Tellegen). The decision was in part conditioned by Film d'Arte's offer to pay her the thirty-thousand dollars which she demanded in order to play the rôle. Director André Calmettes and Henri Pouctal, who was responsible for the scenario, took their stars to Neuilly-sur-Seine for the filming in 1911. They were almost guaranteed a success with the film, for Bernhardt's two tours of the States had already grossed three-million dollars and made her a name that would draw audiences to anything. Sarah did not come before the cameras unprepared, she went to all of the motion pictures companies and studios in Paris and spent hours talking to directors, actors, cameramen. By the time filming started she was an encyclopaedia of information on the art of film-making. A few rehearsals were necessary so that the timing might be accurate, but the filmed version was made in one big 'take' and printed as two reels. Her enthusiasm was considerable and she attended a preview showing with Edmond Rostand. Contrary to reports of her being disappointed and fainting at having overacted, she was delighted with the film and at the finish she turned to Rostand and asked, 'What is next for me?' Further indication of her satisfaction is to be found in a letter which she wrote to her American manager William F. Connor: 'I have conquered a new world – that of the photoplay'. It is interesting that she refers to films as photoplays, for unlike other actresses who adapted to the medium, Sarah initially regarded this technical invention only as a means to record theatre as she knew it. In all her early films she declaimed the French texts just as she would in any theatre. A propos of *La Dame aux camélias* she wrote in her letter to Conner, 'I never thought, my dear William, that I would ever be a film, but now that I am two whole reels of pictures I rely for my immortality on these records.' Of this film *Moving Picture News* of March 1912 contains the following review under the caption 'Sarah the Divine in M.P.'s': 'Camille was never more pitifully eloquent than in this dumb record. She played with wonderful fire and expressiveness. Great genius that she is she suited herself to her medium and the result is a long series of photographs that are staccato in their expressiveness. The story is revealed as plain as print. *Camille* is a perfect photoplay. The story lends itself to the purposes of the camera, and Bernhardt is eloquent in every movement. Someone has said that the pictures fairly crackle with life and project wireless messages to the spectators. All over Europe the photoplay *Camille* is a sensation and Americans are eagerly awaiting the release of these reels, which are now in the control of the French–American Film Company which is rapidly disposing of State rights'. She loathed the use of *Camille* as a title for this film and was heard to remark 'Absurd! Camille is the proper name for a gentleman'. Lou Tellegen is scarcely mentioned in the reviews. His performance is best summarized as embarrassing.

In 1912, at the age of sixty-seven, Bernhardt was convinced by Louis Mercanton that she should appear in the first full-length motion picture as *Elisabeth Reine d'Angleterre*. The play had been written for Sarah by her friend Emile Moreau, who had written *Le Procès de Jeanne d'Arc* for her in 1909. It is surprising that Louis Mercanton, who had invested in a number of French films, was convinced that there was a public for *Elisabeth*. After all, it had lasted only a week in Paris with Sarah in the cast. The supporting cast for the film left much to be desired; Lou Tellegen played Essex with the sameness that had already made him the whipping boy of the critics. Tellegen remembers the original of *Elisabeth* to have been seven consecutive reels; it would be interesting to know if this assertion is correct, for the final version was four reels and there is no record of the additional three. In any case, this was the first full-length film ever made and for it Sarah demanded, and received, three hundred and sixty dollars each day and ten per cent of the gross! This was unheard of, and only so notable a figure as Sarah could have carried off such a coup. She indeed had established the star system. The epic film actually fared well in France, unlike the stage version. Adolph Zukor, who was just starting out in his career, bought the American screening rights for eighteen-thousand dollars. Money was raised by Zukor, Edwin S. Porter, and Joseph Engel (one of the earliest executives of Universal Pictures). Accounts of the transaction vary. According to Mercanton the film was sought after; Zukor relates that it had not yet been completed and was purchased in part to rescue Mercanton from financial ruin. The trio was wise enough to employ Daniel Frohman, brother of the famous Broadway impresario Charles Frohman, to 'present' it; this would ensure an American audience. It is an interesting sign of the confusion of the times that Charles Frohman, unlike his brother, saw motion pictures as a 'trivial passing madness of the masses', and was irritated by his brother's lack of discretion in using the family name. So the

film opened on 12 July 1912 at Broadway's Lyceum Theatre under the auspices of Zukor's Enghandine Company of 'Famous Players in Famous Plays' presented by Daniel Frohman. The epic was well attended by a public who, not having to listen to any spoken French, found it most accessible and stood to cheer her as they had during her stage appearances. Despite a mixed press, this public acclaim resulted in the film being sold for regional distribution for a sum of eight-thousand dollars – a most auspicious beginning. Sarah herself was unworried by the reviews.

An interesting review of *Elisabeth, Reine d'Angleterre* appeared in *The Theatre Magazine* of 1912. The novel production was referred to as a 'remarkable moving picture exhibition of a photoplay in 21 scenes'. The camera was a 'mechanical contrivance' and the projector a 'cinematograph'. In spite of these curious descriptions, the anonymous

Elisabeth Reine d'Angleterre: The Queen is told that her lover Essex is a traitor

Elisabeth Reine d'Angleterre: This photograph was used to produce the first motion picture poster

reviewer was optimistic about the fate of the 'poor man's theatre', for he felt that the film would lead to better theatre through competition with the stage. He also believed that the curse of speechlessness might be removed and the moving picture might someday talk, 'but when it does, it will only be seen in expensive places that will not be common over the country'. As to Bernhardt's performance, he notes that the Divine Sarah, 'did not merely pose mechanically for a mechanical contrivance, but proceeded to give one of the finest performances of which this greatest living artist is capable'. He was especially impressed with her slow sinuous walk. A recent history of the motion picture industry includes only a brief reference to Sarah Bernhardt which states that in *Elisabeth* she hobbled her way through the rôle on a wooden leg. It was not until three years later that Sarah had her leg amputated and afterwards she continued to act by clever placement and carriage, and certainly never 'hobbled' through any rôle.

Elisabeth was followed in 1912 by an offer from Mercanton to film *Adrienne Lecouvreur*. The Scribe and Legouve version of this legend was filmed, although it is said that 'Madame adapted the story for moving picture representation'. The film was brief (1,783 feet) and did not create much critical controversy, in fact it didn't excite much more than one critic's comment that 'historical personages were happily rendered'. The public adored Bernhardt in death scenes so it was a box-office success if only for that. As the eighteenth century actress Adrienne, Sarah had Henri Desfontaines (of *La Dame aux camélias*) as

Madame at home in her salon

her co-star. Directed by Louis Mercanton as a part of the Film d'Arte
series, it was released in America as *Adrienne Lecouvreur, An Actress's
Romance Under Louis XV, in Three Parts.* It was later released simply as
An Actress's Romance.

The whole world was interested in this rare creature whose life and
exploits were known to them through film, tours, biographies and her
own autobiography. If press coverage was so well received, it seemed
logical to make a film of Sarah in her Brittany island. Who could resist
being invited into the home of a woman who was the world's foremost
actress, a painter and sculptress of considerable talent, a keeper of wild
beasts (including a python that devoured all the pillows in her drawing
room and a cheetah that terrorized her dogs). What was the secret of a
woman close to seventy who could give a convincing performance as
L'Aiglon, the young nephew of Napoleon, or who could in middle-age
have faced an audience as Saint Joan and declare her age to be nineteen?
The two-reel documentary film *Sarah Bernhardt at Home* was made in
1912 by Film d'Arte. It provided intimate glimpses into the life of La
Grande Sarah as she wished the public to see it. Among the rocky

149

heights Sarah is seen leading a retinue of devotees including Sir Basil Zaharof and her son Maurice who pants and wipes his brow as the undaunted Sarah continues the climb. Local fishermen whom Sarah befriended during periods of near famine offer homage to her. Instead of the opulent salons of Paris, the viewer is offered a series of vignettes showing her up at dawn to look after the lobster pots, feeding chickens, ducks, geese and pigs with her own hands. Lunches with her family show the gracious Sarah at her best. She appears as a sportswoman fishing in estate pools stocked for her. Tennis matches, while remarkable for a women of her age, are more remarkable when one considers that her crippled leg gave relentless pain. Of course no one was allowed to beat her at tennis or she would pout for days and the entire island retinue would suffer a brief excommunication. Whatever the public expected from *Sarah Bernhardt at Home*, they were rewarded with intimate glimpses, contrived and sentimental though they may be, into a woman with a remarkable style of living.

At home

'Quand Même'

During her American tours Lucien Guitry managed Sarah's theatre and was successful enough in his choice of plays to allow Sarah to return in a new production and not have to stage a revival of one of the public's favourites. Tristan Bernard had written a fine tragedy, *Jeanne Doré*, in which there was not a great deal of stage movement. It was at the thirtieth performance of this play on 15 January that Sarah received the medal of the Légion d'honneur, and few better personified the great spirit of the French.

Jeanne Doré was brought back when Sarah could no longer move about in her March revival of *La Dame aux camélias* and the brief *Tout-à-coup* by Paul and Guy Cassagnac had proved a failure. She could no longer stand without support, and yet in May, Sarah set out for a tour of France. Sarah returned from Lille to Paris, with the declaration of a general mobilization on 1 August 1914, but now the leg would not bend, it was swollen and gangrenous. The baths of ether and injections of morphine had not helped.

By the end of August, Paris was not safe and Sarah and her family were warned of the impending disasters. Sarah was on the list of hostages to be deported if the Germans took Paris. On 31 August she left by car for Andernos, twenty-five miles from Bordeaux. Her leg was now in plaster and immobile; nothing could relieve the pain. Professor Pozzi came from Paris to examine it. Some reports said that it was tubercular. When asked whether it could be saved the doctors said no. Sarah herself then spoke up and said, 'Do what is necessary'. At

Jeanne Doré Tristan Bernard: Jeanne at the prison door keeps a terrible secret from her son (1916)

seventy years of age Sarah was not without courage. She cabled Mrs Patrick Campbell, then in Philadelphia, 'Doctor will cut off my leg next Monday. Am very happy. Kisses. All my heart – Sarah'. The operation was carried out at Dax in the Landes district.

By October Sarah bravely returned to Paris and arranged for a series of performances. She played a scenic poem *Les Cathédrales* and some brief matinee performances. Funds were dwindling and she was forced to sell property and jewellery and take out loans. It was still necessary

to support Maurice and his family, to maintain a staff of servants, and to keep the property at Belle-Isle. In the back of her mind a tour was taking shape. At the same time Sarah was beginning to think about immortalizing herself on film in her greatest rôle, *L'Aiglon*. She wrote to Edmond Rostand, whose work she had previously recorded (the Wagram Plain Scene), and spoke of the undertaking and profits to be made on such a film venture. After all, this was the rôle that left the public of Paris cheering and sobbing – it could not but succeed on film. Desperation coupled with pain led her to discuss the monetary complexities with her lawyer Maître Clunet who in turn contacted Edmond Rostand at Cambo, presenting Sarah's proposals for cinematographic rights and for sharing the takings. This began a war between old friends fraught with misunderstandings, punctuated with gifts of baskets of fruits and flowers. Unfortunately the correspondence received by Rostand is not intact and we can only guess at the exchange. Rostand's lawyer suggested that he defend himself against Madame Bernhardt's excessive demands, but the poet refused, relinquishing all rights for filming to Sarah in order to prevent her from any further distress. He wrote to his lawyer an abnegation stating, 'I gratefully kiss her fingers from which a writ has for me the grace of a lily'. Sarah, tired of feuding with a friend so dear to her and so generous, wrote to her own lawyer saying, 'I do not want to send any more blue lilies to my poet' and added that she would not accept a proferred two thousand francs from him. As to the reasons for the last offer we may only guess. The 'little war of the lilies' was over, and so was the projected cinematic presentation of Sarah in her finest rôle. Under the circumstances the film was best forgotten and Sarah retired to the Boulevard Pereire.

Meanwhile, war was still raging in France in 1915, and as propaganda for the war effort Sarah participated in a film entitled *Les Mères françaises* directed again by her old associate Louis Mercanton and written by Jean Richepin. This story dealing with courageous nurses at the front lines had a distinguished cast of Raymond Bernard, Signoret Gabriel, Louise Lagrange, Berthe Jalabert, and support in direction from René Hervil. The film reappeared as a propaganda piece under such titles as *Maids of France*, *Women of France* and *Heroes of France*. But more dramatic than the film itself was the appearance of Sarah at the front lines in 1916 to perform in the Théâtre aux Armées. Accepting no false limbs, Sarah would either be strategically placed upon a stage or would be carried in on a litter in regal splendour. Needless to say she was an inspiration to thousands of French soldiers who could for a moment forget their own wounds and admire this indomitable woman. Sarah was already busy on the film version of *Jeanne Doré*,

once more directed by Mercanton of Film d'Arte. This rather morbid drama concerns the mother of a man accused of murdering the seducer of his beloved. In the final act Sarah, as the mother, enacted one of her greatest scenes in which she speaks to her son through a prison door, and is mistaken for his beloved; the poignantly portrayed deceit allows the son to go to his death reassured of the love he thought lost.

Sarah was interviewed by H. H. Van Loan concerning this production. Her comments further substantiate the confidence which she had in cinema as the dominant emerging art form. 'The eye', relates Sarah, 'is the mirror of the brain, and the cinema has given to eye-play an infinitely greater scope, power, and importance. A true artist needs no audience to assist her art.' While New York was staging an exhibition entitled 'The Divine Sarah', a private showing of *Jeanne Doré* was screened in Paris amid praise for the subtlety with which she rendered the part. Not only critics were pleased with the motion picture, but Sarah herself voiced her approval. Carl Laemmle, president of Universal Film Manufacturing Company which had been responsible for the u.s. release was so convinced of the success of Bernhardt on film that he stated, 'I am convinced that Sarah Bernhardt will never be seen in the flesh on the stage again'. Sarah had been close to death only months before she embarked on this rôle, and while she did not appear haggard, the pain and suffering was apparent – all too appropriately to the part. At seventy-one Sarah worked with the vitality and energy of a young actress, even though it is reported that she went directly from the hospital to the studio to accomplish this film. She oversaw every detail and now had an excellent sense of cinema. She appeared in over one hundred scenes and because of her amputation it was necessary for her to position herself strategically. With her old friends in the cast, Mlle Seylor as Mme Tissot, Mlle Costa as Louise, and M. Raymond Bernard as Jacques Doré she was in familiar company. Sarah was constantly instructing them on cinematic deportment.

Sarah reportedly found it a distinct help to be supported by 'real scenery' in moving pictures. She enjoyed the brevity of each scene which allowed 'the faculties to be concentrated to a much higher degree than on stage'. A peculiar comment in light of present film making is the following: 'Another feature about moving pictures which strikes me favourably is that once a scene has been acted and taken, repetition is unnecessary. After having repeated performances many hundreds of times, I find the variety and change of moving picture acting an excellent mental stimulant.' While these comments were directed toward the production of *Jeanne Doré*, they capture Sarah's basic attitudes toward cinema as it existed in 1916.

Les Mères Françaises Jean Richepin: Sarah, the courageous nurse, reminds a soldier of the heroism of Jeanne d'Arc and his duty to France

Final Years

In the year 1916 with ten countries at war there was no alternative but to leave for yet another American 'farewell tour'. Would they accept a seventy-two year old one-legged woman as anything more than a curiosity? These thoughts troubled Sarah, but did not alter her decision. On 30 September she embarked with only ten actors in her company (usually there were thirty). She determined that it was not necessary to do complete plays, she would do scenes from her greatest successes and supplement them with a few brief additions. In this way she could overcome her physical limitations. This time Sarah played at many new theatres, many of them vaudeville, and on more than one occasion she found herself sandwiched between vaudeville acts. Charles Frohman managed this tour for Sarah, and the publicity was good, but as her greatest rôles were now out of the question, when she left New York on 1 January 1918, one and a half years later, it was not a triumphant departure.

During this Farewell to America Tour of 1916–18 Sarah was persuaded by Vocalion Discs to record Louis Paven's poem *La Prière pour nos ennemis* and *L'Etoile dans la nuit* by Emile Guérinon and Henri Cain. At this time Sarah was seventy-four years of age. She was constantly in pain and yet her voice seems unaffected. Even more evident is the precise articulation, the balance between force and volume, and the caressing of each word in a punctilious fashion. The tremulo in Paven's poem is heartrending in effect. Sarah was in full command of her magnificent voice and was prepared to accept or

Sarah near the end of her career

Sarah on her final American
tour (1916–1918)

reject rules of prosody as her intuition dictated. While adhering to the author's punctuation in *La Prière pour nos ennemis* Sarah established her own cadences and chose to pronounce or eliminate traditionally mute syllables as they suited her conception of style within a single line of the poem. These final recordings were a satisfactory culmination of a tradition and marked a severance from the bondage of formal dramatic declamation.

During the next few years Sarah continued in her established repertoire and added occasional new rôles as favours to friends. The traditional rôles were now reduced to scenes only so that Sarah was not forced to stand for more than a few moments, and these tableaux were accomplished by carefully positioned props. Wigs covered the white hair that was formerly rinsed with henna, and Sarah's cosmetics became more exaggerated to compensate for the ravages of severe progressive poisoning.

Until 1920 only a few sporadic performances of *Athalie* and *Vitrail* were seen in Paris, the former only at classical matinees and the latter enjoying only fourteen performances. Then it was announced that on 9 November 1920 Sarah would appear in a full-length new work *Daniel*, by her friend Louis Verneuil. During the first two acts of the play Sarah was not on stage; in the last two she was seen as a noble-hearted gentleman aged about thirty, addicted to morphine. Before the opening night, the newspapers asked that no person attend without bringing at least one flower for Sarah who for so many years had been absent from the stage. Two-thousand people crowded into the Théâtre Sarah Bernhardt. When the curtain rose on the third act the audience at last saw their Sarah and for ten minutes called her name. She stood to bow, concealing her amputation. The audience applauded her delivery during the performance and then at the end a storm of flowers filled the stage. The play filled the theatre for three months. Sarah was heartened and staged a benefit performance of *Comment on écrit l'histoire* for an actor friend who had not had work for two years. By April Sarah had the courage to take *Daniel* to London for two weeks at the Princes Theatre, and then on to Madrid and Barcelona. This was followed by a tour through the south of France giving lectures and poetry readings. Each lecture lasted almost two and a half hours, lest anyone question the endurance of Sarah at the age of seventy-seven. But as summer came it was pleasant to retire to Belle-Isle. Here she had an opportunity to read the proposed series of tableaux entitled *La Glorie* presented to her by Maurice Rostand, son of Edmond. Maurice adored Sarah to the extent that he had his hair curled and dyed to resemble hers, and even his face was made up like Sarah's. Maurice proposed that Sarah

Athalie Racine: Sarah is seated next to Marguerite Moreno who appeared with her in this late production (1922)

161

Athalie: Sarah in her dressing room before a performance

Daniel Louis Verneuil: '... an obliterating experience'

present these tableaux behind a scrim upon which was painted Glory, an allegorical figure, dressed in a red and gold gown and crowned in laurel. In each of the three tableaux the dark cabinet in which Glory (Sarah) was seated would become illuminated and she would recite her lines – only about a hundred in total. The play ran from 19 October to mid December. Critics attacked it as an impoverished play, but by this

time Sarah was extremely ill with intermittent attacks of uremic poisoning. She was constantly suffering from a lowering of temperature and had to be wrapped in furs and hot water bottles whenever she was not on stage.

However, she was to fight on to the end so it would be *en scene* that she would die as she had said so many years earlier. In spite of her worsening condition, she persisted in undertaking in 1922 another strenuous European tour which took her to Belgium, Holland, Switzerland and back to France. During this tour she re-enacted her own life in an eerie play by Louis Verneuil called *Régine Armand*.

It should not have been necessary for La Grande Sarah to do any acting late in life; on her American tours alone she made nearly six-million dollars in gold, but this sum was spent as quickly as it was earned. Driven by her compulsion to sustain the legend as well as to pay her own way through life, Sarah announced in 1922 that she would appear as a clairvoyante in Films Abdoré's production of *La Voyante*, a film whose author is unknown, with Sacha Guitry, Harry Baur, Lily Damita, Mary Marquet, Georges Melchoir, François Fratellini, Mme. Paquerette, Raymond Agnel and Alphonse Gibor. It did not take the power of a clairvoyant to ascertain that Bernhardt was in the process of dying. (Unknown to Sarah, an actress by the name of Jeanne Brindeau was called in as a surrogate and was ultimately to finish this film with her back to the cameras.) The Press seized upon the situation, producing such grotesque headlines as the following from the *Boston Sunday Advertiser* of 18 March 1923, 'Bernhardt, Dying, Acts for Movies'.

It is true that at this period Sarah was in financial difficulties and needed all the revenues that such a film might provide. She had never required the support of others and was too proud to accept it now when she was so near death. Promotional advertising seemed premature, but she allowed herself to be photographed at her house in Paris with her favourite chimpanzee. Filming began in a studio in Paris, but by mid-March Sarah was so ill that she requested that the company continue working in her home on the Boulevard Pereire. Her eyes were so weakened by the spreading poison in her system that she had to wear dark glasses between takes. A few frames of this film reveal a corpse-like figure bent over tarot cards, the effect heightened by the kohl beneath her eyes. On 22 March after several relapses into coma had interrupted filming, the indefatigable Sarah announced, 'They can now film me in bed'. A backcloth of Paris was placed in the room and the company continued against the wishes of all but the magnificent and heroic Bernhardt.

Sarah was beyond receiving company and wished only to be able to complete her film. However there was one person for whom an exception had to be made – Nellie Melba. Sarah had performed with Melba *La Ballade du déspére* in the salon of Lady George Cooper when they were both on tour in America. When Melba knew of Sarah's impending death she hastened to Paris to see her one last time. Not to be seen as a defeated woman, Sarah prepared herself carefully for the meeting, trying to appear gay and well. Pink roses were placed on her writing desk and Sarah dressed attractively, rouged her white cheeks and drew on the thick dark red lips of her youth; a flurry of blonde hair crowned this masterpiece of artifice. Melba came into the library astonished to see her friend seeming quite well and poured forth a mellifluous greeting. Sarah's eyes clouded and tears melted the kohl beneath them. A thin quavering voice sobbed, '. . . Ah Melba, you still have your golden voice. My golden voice no longer needs me because I am dying'. Curiously her reference to that voice was in the third person as though the voice with a life of its own had already found repose elsewhere. Sarah had always regarded it as a gift of God and now it had gone forever, leaving behind only vestiges of that vibrant sound recorded in the surfaces of cylinders and discs.

On the following day it was no longer possible to continue filming. It was spring in Paris and Sarah asked her son, Maurice, to cover her with roses, lilacs and Parma violets. A priest was brought to administer the last rights, and at five past eight in the evening of 25 March, Sarah's life-long dream was realized 'to become a legend during my lifetime, and not to be dead before dying'.

The life that Edmond de Goncourt, foremost chronicler of the late nineteenth century had described as, 'the most remarkable phenomenon of the nineteenth century' had come to an end. Eight films and about a dozen recordings preserve for us the visage and golden voice that dominated the world stage for almost sixty years.

Appendix

List of principal plays in which Sarah Bernhardt acted.

(The part, when possible, is indicated in brackets.)

Comédie Française
Iphigénie (Iphigénie). Racine. 11 August 1862.
Valérie (Valérie). 24 August 1862.
Les Femmes Savantes (Henriette). Molière. 12 September 1862.
L'Étourdi (Hippolyte). Molière. 6 March 1863.

Gymnase
Le Père de la Débutante (Anita). Théodore Barrière.
Le Démon du Jeu.
Un Soufflet n'est Jamais Perdu.
La Maison sans Enfants. Dumanoir.
L'Étourneau. Bayard and Laya.
Le Premier Pas. Labiche and Delacour.
Un Mari Qui Lance sa Femme. Reymond Deslandes.

Porte Saint-Martin
La Biche Aux Bois (Princess Desirée).
Les Femmes Savantes (Armande). Molière.

Odéon
Le Jeu de L'Amour et du Hasard. Marivaux.
Britannicus (Junie). Racine.

Le Marquis de Villemer. Georges Sand.
François le Champi (Mariette). Georges Sand.
Athalie (Zacharie). Racine.
Le Testament de César Girodot (Hortense). Balzac.
Kean (Anna Damby). Alexandre Dumas *père*.
Le Roi Lear (Cordelia). Shakespeare.
Le Legs.
Le Drame de la Rue de la Paix. Adolphe Belot. 1869.
La Gloire de Molière. Th. de Banville.
Le Passant (Zanetto). François Coppée. 1869.
Le Batard. Alphonse Touroude.
L'Autre. Georges Sand. September 1869.
Jean-Marie. André Theuriet. 1871.
La Baronne. C. and E. Foussier.
Mlle. Aïssé (Mlle. Aïssé). Louis Bouilhet. January 1872.
Ruy Blas (La Reine). Victor Hugo. 1872.

Comédie Française
Mlle. de Belle-Isle. Dumas *père*. 6 November 1872.
Britannicus (Junie). Racine. 14 December 1872.
Le Mariage de Figaro (Cherubin). Beaumarchais. 30 January 1873.
Dalila (La Princesse Falconieri). Octave Feuillet. 28 March 1873.
Andromaque (Andromaque). Racine. 22 August 1873.
Phèdre (Aricie). Racine. 17 September 1873.
Le Sphinx. Octave Feuillet. 23 March 1874.
L'Absent. Eugène Manuel.   ⎱ One act. 1873.
Chez l'Avocat. Paul Ferrier.   ⎰
Zaïre. Voltaire. 6 August 1874.
La Belle Paule. Louis Denayrouse. One act. 1874.
Phèdre (Phèdre). Racine. 21 December 1874.
La Fille de Roland (Berthe). Henri de Bornier. 15 February 1875.
Gabrielle. Émile Augier. 1875.
L'Étrangère (Mistress Clarkson). A. Dumas *fils*. 14 February 1876.
Rome Vaincue (Posthumia). Parodi. 27 September 1876.
Hernani (Doña Sol). Victor Hugo. 21 November 1877.
Amphitryon (Alcmène). Molière. 2 April 1878.
Mithridate (Monime). Racine. 7 February 1879.
Ruy Blas (Maria de Neubourg). Victor Hugo. 4 April 1879.
L'Aventurière (Doña Clorinde). Émile Augier. 17 April 1880.
Andrienne Lecouvreur. London. 1880.
Froufrou. London. 1880.
Les Enfants d'Édouard. Delavigne. London. 1880.
American tour: *La Princesse Georges*. Dumas *fils*. New York. 1880.
La Dame Aux Camélias. Dumas *fils*. London 1881.
Fédora. Sardou. Vaudeville, Paris. 12 December 1882.
Nana Sahib. Richepin. Porte Saint-Martin. 1883.
Macbeth. Shakespeare. Porte Saint-Martin. 1883.
Théodora. Sardou. Porte Saint-Martin. 1884.
Marion Delorme. Victor Hugo. Porte Saint-Martin. 31 December 1885.
Hamlet (Ophelia). Shakespeare. Porte Saint-Martin. 7 February 1886.

American and South American tour, lasting thirteen months. 1886.
La Tosca. Sardou. Porte Saint-Martin. 1887.
La Tosca. Sardou. Lyceum, London. 1888.
Françillon. Dumas *fils.* Lyceum, London, 1888.
European tour: Turkey, Egypt. 1888.
Léna. F. C. Phillips. Variétés. 1889.
Jeanne d'Arc. Barbier. Porte Saint-Martin. 1890.
Cléopâtre. Sardou and Moreau. Porte Saint-Martin. January 1890–91.
Pauline Blanchard.
La Dame de Chalant.
Tour in Australia: *Pauline Blanchard.* Sydney. 1891.
Tour in Europe and South America. 1892.

Théâtre de La Renaissance
Management of Madame Sarah Bernhardt from November 1893 to January
1899.

1893
Les Rois. Jules Lemaître. 5 November.
Phèdre. Racine.
La Dame aux Camélias. A. Dumas *fils.*
Izeïl. Armand Silvestre. With Lucien Guitry.
Fédora (Revival). Victorian Sardou. With Guitry.
La Femme de Claude. A. Dumas *fils.*

1894
Gismonda. Victorien Sardou. With De Max and Guitry.
Amphitryon. Molière.
Magda. Sudermann.
Jean-Marie. Theuriet.
La Princesse Lointaine. E. Rostand.
Lorenzaccio. Adapted from Musset by Dartois.
Spiritisme. Victorien Sardou. (With Abel Deval).
La Tosca (Revival). Victorien Sardou. (With Abel Deval as Scarpia).
La Samaritaine. E. Rostand.
Les Mauvais Bergers. Octave Mirbeau.
La Ville Morte. Gabriele d'Annunzio.
Lysiane. Romain Coolus.
Médée. Catulle Mendès.

Théâtre Sarah Bernhardt
Management of Madame Sarah Bernhardt from January 1899
to March 1923.
1899
La Tosca (Revival). Victorien Sardou.
Phèdre. Racine.
Dalila. Octave Feuillet.
La Samaritaine. Edmond Rostand.
La Dame Aux Camélias. A. Dumas *fils.*
Hamlet. Translated by Marcel Schwob.

1900
L'Aiglon. Edmond Rostand.

1901
Cyrano de Bergerac. (Roxane). London.

1902
Théodora (Revival). Victorien Sardou.
La Femme de Claude. A. Dumas *fils*.
Jean-Marie. Theuriet.
Magda. Sudermann.
Phèdre. Racine.
La Samaritaine. Edmond Rostand.
Francesca da Rimini. Marion Crawford.
Fédora (Revival). Victorien Sardou.
Théroigne de Méricourt. Paul Hervieu.

1903
Andromaque (Hermione). Racine.
Werther. Pierre Decourcelle.
La Légende du Coeur. Jean Aicart.
Jane Wedeking.
La Sorcière. Victorien Sardou.

1904
Le Festin de la Mort. Marquis de Castellanne.
Bohemos. Miguel Zamaçois.
Varennes. Lenôtre and Lavedan.
Angelo. Victor Hugo.
Esther. Racine.

1905
Pelléas et Mélisande. Maeterlinck. (London, with Mrs. Patrick Campbell).

1906
La Vierge D'Avila. Catulle Mendès.

1907
Les Bouffons. Miguel Zamaçois.
Adrienne Lecouvreur. Sarah Bernhardt.
La Belle au Bois Dormant. Jean Richepin and Henri Cain.

1908
Cléonice. Michel Carré and Bilhaud.

1909
La Fille de Rabenstein. Paul Remon.
Le Procès de Jeanne D'Arc. Émile Moreau.

1910
La Beffa. Benelli and Jean Richepin.
Le Bois Sacré. Edmond Rostand.
La Conquête D'Athènes. Albert du Bois.

1911
Lucrèce Borgia. Victor Hugo.

1912
La Reine Élisabeth. Émile Moreau.
Lorenzaccio. Musset and Dartois.

1913
Jeanne Doré. Tristan Bernard.
Tout à Coup. de Cassagnac.

1915
Les Cathédrales.

1920
Athalie. Racine.
Daniel. Louis Verneuil.

1921
La Gloire. Maurice Rostand.
Comment on Écrit L'Histoire. Sacha Guitry.

1922
Régine Armand. Louis Verneuil.
La Voyante

Bibliography

Agate, May *Madame Sarah* New York: Benjamin Blom, Inc., 1945; London: Home & Van Thal Ltd., 1945

Arthur, George *Sarah Bernhardt* New York: Doubleday Page & Co., 1923

Baring, Maurice *Sarah Bernhardt* New York: Benjamin Blom, Inc., 1933; London: Peter Davies Ltd., 1933

Binet-Valmer *Sarah Bernhardt* Paris: Flammarion, 1936

Bernhardt, Lysiane *Sarah Bernhardt ma Grand'mère* Paris: Editions du Pavois, 1947

Bernhardt, Sarah *Memories of My Life* New York: Benjamin Blom, Inc., 1968.

Buson, Dani *Sarah Bernhardt* Paris: Publications Willy Fischer

Campbell, Beatrice *My Life and Some Letters* London: Hutchinson & Co.

Castelot, André *Sarah Bernhardt* Paris: Le Livre Contemporain, 1961

Colombier, Marie *Les Mémoires de Sarah Barnum* Paris

Geller, G. G. *Sarah Bernhardt Divine Eccentric* New York: Benjamin Blom, Inc., 1933

Hahn, Reynaldo *La Grande Sarah* New York: Benjamin Blom, Inc., Paris: Hachette, 1930

Hart, Jerome A. *Sardou and the Sardou Plays* Philadelphia: J. B. Lippincott & Co., 1913

Huret, Jules *Sarah Bernhardt* Paris: 1899

Lanco, Yvonne *Belle-Isle-en-Mer, Sarah Bernhardt Souvenirs* Paris: Les Nouvelles Editions Debresse, 1961

Melba, Nellie *Melodies and Memories* New York: AMS Press, Inc., 1926

Robertson, W. Graham *Life Was Worth Living* New York: Harper & Bros., 1931

Rostand, Maurice *Sarah Bernhardt* Paris: Calmann-Levy, 1950

Row, Arthur William *Sarah the Divine* New York: Comet Press Books, 1957

Rueff, Suzie *I Knew Sarah Bernhardt* London: Frederick Miller Ltd., 1951

Skinner, Cornelia Otis *Madame Sarah* Boston: Houghton Mifflin Co., 1967; London: Michael Joseph, 1967

Taranow, Gerda *Sarah Bernhardt, the Art within the Legend* Princeton: Princeton University Press, 1972

Tellegen, Lou *Women Have Been Kind* New York: Vanguard Press, 1931

Verneuil, Louis *La Vie Merveillieuse de Sarah Bernhardt* New York: Bretano's, 1942

Woon, Basil *The Real Sarah Bernhardt* New York: Boni and Liveright, 1924

Index

173

174